David Gentleman's Coastline

Walton-on-the-Naze

Hunstanton

David Gentleman's Coastline

Weidenfeld & Nicolson
London

Author's note
I would like to thank John Curtis, Candida Brazil,
Richard Hussey, George Sharpe, Douglas Matthews and Gertrud Watson
for their help in preparing this book for press.

Endpapers: cast iron railing, Brighton Palace Pier

for Tom

First published in Great Britain in 1988 by
George Weidenfeld & Nicolson Limited
91 Clapham High Street, London sw4 7ta

ISBN 0 297 79314 4

Illustration separations by Newsele Litho
Filmset by Keyspools Limited, Golborne, Lancs
Printed in Italy by LEGO Vicenza

Contents

Introduction

Going to the seaside is the first experience I can properly remember. It was an unforgettable moment when the road from the station, which had seemed to end abruptly in empty sky, fell away to reveal the magically straight and level line of the sea's distant horizon. Beneath it lay the waves and the beach of hard-packed sand, divided by dark wooden groynes running straight out into the water. Just across the road from the beach was a terrace of four or five houses; one of these was Mrs Drew's boarding-house. Everything about this house seemed to me very odd. The dining-room had an aspidistra plant in a pot, many layers of thick cloth on the table, and a jigsaw puzzle: a scene of snow-covered houses with yellow lamplit windows. My bedroom had a chamber-pot and a heavily curtained sash window that wouldn't slide up and down; it looked straight out on to the sea.

The beach was reached by way of stone or wooden ramps sloping down from the esplanade, which was fenced with heavy green cast-iron railings. Down on the sand there were tin buckets and wooden spades, streams and pools and wormcasts and the smell of seaweed; and there were newly made friends, the Blacks and the Harrops, who were staying in other nearby boarding-houses. My father would dig holes and build sandcastles with me while my mother tried to shelter from the east-coast wind against one of the groynes. Sometimes, to my dismay, they would abandon me to play grown-up games with a quoit or a hand-ball, on a squarish court newly scratched out on the sand with their toes; jealously I tried to rub these lines out. I know from old snapshots that my mother had a straw hat with a wide brim and that my father wore a 1930s bathing costume with shoulder straps, though I'd never have remembered such things. But I can remember very clearly how when he went swimming I would cling piggy-back to him in the odd-tasting waves.

At the top of the beach was a steeply sloping seawall made of rough boulders; since this was easy to climb up but hard to climb down, I had to be rescued frequently. A little way up the beach was a long wooden pier. You could trundle to its far end on an open tramway, or you could walk it, past groups of anglers whose rods had little round bells at their tips which jingled if they caught anything. If you peered down through the cracks between the deck timbers you could see the heaving waves. A paddle-steamer with a black-and-yellow funnel sailed from the far end of the pier, left to Felixstowe, right to Clacton or even to London. Or you could get to Frinton under your own steam – a country walk along low cliffs topped by grass, called the Greensward. My father and I sometimes used to make this walk in the morning after collecting the terrier Dan from his overnight imprisonment in the town kennels. On the way back my father would point out the projecting headland, like a snout sticking out into the North Sea, that gave Walton-on-the-Naze its name. Walton must, I suppose, have been cold and windy and occasionally very boring, but if so I've forgotten. I can only remember loving the place, assuming that this was what all seaside towns were like, and wanting, after each visit, to go back there.

Not long ago I did go back, after a gap of over fifty years. It was not much different from what I remembered: a pretty little town still complete with a working railway station, a Martello tower, an Old and a New Pier Street and a Marine Parade. The seafront was run down but not too tarted up. Some of the terrace I remembered had gone, but a bed-and-breakfast still stood on Marine Parade in roughly the same place as Mrs Drew's boarding-house; that is, in the stretch remaining between Steve's Takeaway and the foundations of a new hotel on the one hand and a concrete public lavatory of the locked-up-till-the-season variety on the other. The terrace's own front gardens had become concrete car-stands but there was a walled patch of municipal grass landscaping in front. On the esplanade below it a Walls van was delivering ice-cream to a neat little café whose front was ablaze with bright plastic buckets and spades and whirling windmills. The cast-iron work had gone and an almost vertical concrete seawall, perfectly smooth and clinical, had replaced the rough sloping stonework I'd once clambered up; but small family groups still huddled for shelter against the wooden groynes. Thinnish spreading stains of brown sediment discoloured the beach, and a large expanded polystyrene box, once used to pack some piece of electrical equipment, bobbed weightlessly on the wavelets.

The long straight wooden pier was as splendid and as solid as ever, and as I walked its stoutly timbered length in the spring sunlight and the light breeze Walton suddenly seemed almost unchanged. Towards the far end the pier alters course several degrees to the south and widens out, the pattern of the deck timbers growing more complicated.

ton · on · the · Naze

Half a dozen anglers were the only other people there, with longer and more flexible rods than those I remembered, two or more apiece; now and again they landed dabs, eels, and small codling which they posted back into the water through the slits between the deck planking. There were no steamers of course, but the heavy iron bollards they had once tied up at were still there. Grass grew between the timbers. Down the coast in the warm sea haze you could see the high-rise flats of Frinton, and the unbroken ribbon of sixties bungalows that now connects it to Walton; on the beach beneath the thin greensward strip were many ranks of newish beach huts. It was very peaceful. The only sounds were the whirring of the fishermen's reels and the broken snatches of their conversation, the gentle slap of waves on the wooden piles, the occasional distant thunder of high explosive from the Foulness ranges and the periodic ear-splitting roar and whine of a jet fighter hurtling low along the coast. But back on the landward end of the pier were two white sheds, as big and as pretty as aircraft hangars, full of Amusements. Over their doors were crudely executed signs advertising Burgers, Donuts and Soft Ice, Popcorn and Bowling and Bingo. The largest sign of all read

WALTON PIER
THE HAPPIEST SOUND ON ALL THE EARTH
IS THAT OF CHILDREN'S LAUGHTER

Inside, the only laughter you could hear came from the electronic depths of Popeye the Sailor.

The coastline is made up of white cliffs and pink flesh, lobster pots and nuclear power-stations, double yellow lines and no vacancies, lighthouses and landladies, limitless distances and tiny pebbles, cafés and pubs and terraces and piers, trips round the island and sun-whitened timbers; all of them good to look at and good to draw.

Over the last year or two I've had another look at most of the seaside places I knew in the past; not out of nostalgia but from curiosity and in the course of a broad look at the coastline as a whole. This book is arranged as an anti-clockwise progression round the shore of Britain, beginning in Essex and finishing in Kent; in it I've concentrated more on the things that seemed vivid and curious than on those that were attractive or 'beautiful'.

Many of the things I saw were familiar and unaltered, durable and timeless; scenes and objects that my grandparents would have recognized. On the beaches, now as in the past, there are boats and winches, nets and cables and anchors, groynes and beach huts; on the jetties, lobster pots and fish boxes, floats and marker buoys and lime-kilns; beyond high-water mark there are the same esplanades, railings, steps, terraces, pubs, bandstands and cliff railways, pleasure gardens, boat trips to the island, outings to the ruined castle and to the lighthouse, bucket-and-spade and souvenir shops, donkey rides and fishing from the pier.

I also came across many things that would have seemed strange and unrecognizable even thirty years ago, but which now already seem familiar and inevitable elements of the coastline: inflatables; plastic buoys and nets; marinas and holiday villages; converted warehouses, deserted ports, abandoned industries; broken piers, filled-in docks and empty fishing harbours; seashore petro-chemical plants and oil and gas terminals; oil-rig construction sites, and the rigs themselves out on the horizon or laid up in the inlets; power-stations, both nuclear and conventional; silent shipyards, monster conference centres, car parks and caravan sites. There is also a new and pervasive spirit: a recently arrived reverence for anything which, no longer working in its own right, can be refurbished and labelled 'Heritage'.

Not surprisingly in such a long coastline I found extreme differences. Places in the north and west of Scotland so thinly populated that I felt like the first person to tread there, crowded places on the south coast where it seemed almost as though some great city had been cut in two and both halves dumped side by side on the shore; Sunderland where the shipping industry and the town's livelihood had vanished, and Barrow-in-Furness which was doing very nicely; the Farne Islands where every crumb of flat surface was covered with cormorants, and Blackpool where every crumb was packed with people; Broadstairs where you could hardly see the sand for bathers, and Caldey Island where the only bathers were seals; places like Druridge Bay where the only things to be seen were sand and sky, and others like Seal Sands where no sand could be seen and where you could hardly see the sky for the chimneys, the pipework and the pylons crisscrossing it.

I enjoy being near the sea for many reasons, some of them probably generally shared, others that may be more familiar to people who enjoy drawing. It is pleasant to wake to the sound of waves on shingle and blackbirds from the cliff; to hear boats puttering out to sea in the dawn; to walk on the jetty and on the beach in the fresh morning; to experience open space and distance, the flatness and the newly minted perfection of the sands; to watch other people at work on tasks one can almost understand, or busy in pursuit of happiness, well-being and a tan.

But drawing an empty beach is more complicated than it looks; it quickly reveals unexpected subtleties. Reflections occur in odd places; wet sand reflects things much better than ruffled pools of water, and a restless dark sea hardly reflects the sky at all. A beach is seldom as bare and level as it looks, being marked by weeds and wormcasts, débris and wavelet patterns, crossed by streams and lagoons, and formed into humps and plateaux and depressions. Beach and sea are sometimes darker than the sky, sometimes lighter; the sea can look like a millpond or a ploughed field; its colour varies as the light strikes down through it to the light sand or is lost in deep water, and as the moving facets of its waves reflect sun, sky or cloud.

Many of the most fascinating things by the sea are things that man has added; and in general they are the subject matter of this book. Almost without exception the traditional working buildings of the seashore look splendid. I have always enjoyed drawing jetties and quayside buildings because of their bold emphatic shapes and simple lines: like the lines of downland. Paul Nash and John Piper and Eric Ravilious, Ben Nicholson, Alfred Wallis and Christopher Wood, all noticed this and turned it to account

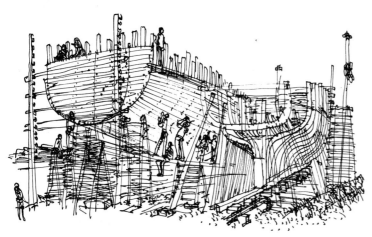

Boatbuilding at Arbroath

in their various ways. Part of the appeal of these structures is their easily understood function: steps for getting into a boat, a harbour entrance white-painted so that seamen can see it in the dark, a box above a row of warehouse doors that contains a pulley, an old goods van that has become a fishermen's storage hut. The simplest structures like harbour walls, breakwaters, jetties and quays, sheds and shelters – things which sometimes seem little more than extensions of natural rock formations – are as impressive as the more complicated things like warehouses and maltings, piers and cranes, lighthouses and docks for which carpenters and builders, engineers and architects have clearly been needed. I like their ordinariness and durability and their worn, tarred or bleached condition, just as I like the blistered tar or the many coats of white paint which hold the fishermen's storage huts together through storm and shine.

And the fishermen's boats, too, are good to look at. Small inshore working boats have remarkably varied shapes, with local characteristics adapted to suit the shores they beach on. The paunchy luggers of Hastings are fat-bellied for stability after they have been winched up on to the steep Sussex shingle; the smaller and lighter shrimp boats of Dunwich are built for the harsh Suffolk beach. The broad-beamed, high-ended crab boats of Sheringham and Cromer seem to sag and flop as they are dragged up on trailers by tractor on to the flatter Norfolk sand; the curious cobles of the north-east, beached high and dry under Flamborough Head or floating in the rudimentary harbours of Staithes or Beadnell, have almost Viking lines. The first time I saw one of these boats being pulled through a Holderness town on its trailer, I thought it was some kind of mistake, an amateurish and misshapen float perhaps from a historical pageant. The Scottish fishing ports have fine sturdy boats: small and wooden at Eyemouth and Arbroath and Stonehaven and on the west coast, bigger metal ones at Peterhead. And although the great traditional fishing fleets of the past – of Brixham, Yarmouth, Grimsby, Fleetwood and the Fife villages – have dwindled or here and there shrunk away almost to nothing, many active small fleets are still sprinkled round the shore, bringing to their harbours and quaysides the fascination of a real working industry.

Where the fishing has dwindled, the empty spaces have been filled by an increasing array of pleasure-craft: fibreglass launches, dinghies and yachts of all kinds, in harbours, on moorings, parked like cars in crowded marinas, or discernible far out at sea, enlivening the horizon with their white sails and the gaiety of their coloured spinnakers bellying out, the whole scene looking as delightful and timeless as it does in the seascapes of the past.

The long thin shape of the map of Britain, like a squeezed toothpaste tube, shows why the country has, for its modest size, such a lot of seashore – the longest stretch of any European country. Its outline, in part crinkly and fissured and crumbling, and in part smooth and unbroken, shows why the coastline is so varied in nature.

All coastal landscape is picturesque, in the true sense of that now disused word: one enjoys it instinctively, without bothering to wonder why. Yet it's easy to see why it delights us. For one thing, it's like a delicious meal which does its own washing up; twice a day it's renewed as fresh and sparkling as a clean tumbler. For another, it always comes in two halves. Whereas any inland landscape surrounds you unbroken, any coastal one is neatly bisected: water and space one way, everything else the other. The spacious half is invariably beautiful, being a blank canvas for the play of light and weather on clouds and water and shimmering beach; and the people and the houses on the seafront face this prospect as if from the circle at the theatre.

There are no Tudor, Jacobean Restoration or early Georgian seaside resorts: only during the last 250 years or so did people start coming to the sea in order to feel healthier or simply to enjoy it. In doing so they managed to create something previously unknown, the Seaside, with all its attendant elegance, oddity and charm. To attract and cater for this taste, obscure fishing villages were transformed and new towns came into being, along with the accommodation, services and amenities the visitors needed. These developments began in various places at different times: at Scarborough in the 1730s, at Brighton by the 1750s, at Margate in the 1770s, Ramsgate and Lowestoft in the 1780s, Southend by the 1790s. Where a royal visit and approval confirmed a resort's popularity, dates are more specific: Sidmouth 1781, Weymouth 1789, Worthing 1798. Thereafter, development as resorts forged ahead as fast as the resources allowed, though now and then ambitious plans (like Robert Adam's idea to develop a spa at Mistley in Essex) petered out. But in general they prospered, until piers and cliff railways, winter gardens and shopping arcades, esplanades and promenades and bandstands, Regency terraces sparkling with cast-ironwork and Victorian terraces gleaming with painted stucco, the heavy iron railings above the beach and the wooden groynes stuck into it, all came to seem as natural a part of the seaside scene as sand and shingle, boulder and cliff. There is a recognizable seaside style – or 'vernacular' as it is grandly called – made up of the agreeable, practical and once unselfconscious usages of harbour and esplanade. This seaside look, identified and championed by John Piper and John Betjeman, a breezy amalgam of marine parade, pier and quarter-deck adopted, was as a useful and cheerful all-purpose style by Hugh Casson and the Festival of Britain designers; and by others after them, even far inland. Indeed, it has survived as a decorative style longer than the originals it was based on, for, at the seaside itself, many of these motifs have been replaced with fibreglass, or are tending simply to disappear, being abandoned, worn out or hard to maintain.

But economic forces are altering the coastline's most familiar sights and activities: even the very ones that first brought it to life. Dockside cranes have vanished as the older ports have emptied or been filled in or become container terminals. The only shipbuilding now in progress on Teeside is the renovation of old submarines, to be sold to foreign navies. Tyneside is building for the Ministry of Defence – a captive market. In Scotland and the north-east, shipbuilding – once their principal industry – has virtually ceased; it is flourishing today only at Barrow-in-Furness where Vickerstown, having built the battleships for both sides in the Falklands War, is supplying the demand for nuclear submarines.

Access to the coast is changing too. Though many of the railways that brought people to the sea have been closed, leaving only ghost stations and the ruins of bridges, motorways have brought the once distant regions of Scotland, Wales and the north of England much nearer: the country now seems smaller than it did. And the scale of the landscape itself has changed: seaside landmarks like lighthouses, cliff-top castles and sometimes even the great cliffs themselves have shrunk to relative insignificance in comparison with power-stations and blocks of high-rise flats. Maintaining things in good order has grown more expensive. Even that seemingly permanent feature of many a seaside town, its pier, has proved vulnerable. Some, like Brighton's pretty West Pier, have simply shut up shop and barricaded themselves away behind barbed wire. Others have been burnt up. Southend's has been chopped in two by a careless ship, and at Herne Bay and Margate only the far end of the old pier remains, marooned far out to sea like a seafort or an oil-rig. Others again have vanished almost entirely, leaving behind only some bizarre detail, like the monumentally arched and turreted gateway at Withernsea which now leads not on to a pier but only on to the empty Holderness beach.

Local individuality too is on the decline. Genuine regional differences are delightful but contrived ones are irritating. Corgis painted on Scottish locomotives, *tacsi* on Welsh cabs, red dragons or Cornish piskies or bits of tartan in the appropriate regions are all trying to disguise the relentless sameness that is creeping in as local industries and customs give way to universal ones. More and more seaside hardware is production-line: the same windmills on the franchised putting-greens, the same shop fascias, the same inflatables and the same ill-modelled fibreglass submarines, tanks and rockets for children to ride on. And as tourism is promoted more and more energetically, the very thing it feeds on – true local character – is being eroded and vulgarized. This is a serious loss, for places appeal to something very deep-rooted in us. I sometimes revisit places

and landscapes in dreams, and feel the same kind of delight and longing for them that one may feel in dreaming of another person. But it's hard to yearn for Macdonalds or Walls or National Car Parks, inflatable Jolly Jumbos or Konkord Kastles, when they are the same everywhere.

On the other hand, the charm and individuality of many resorts have survived. Lovely places like Whitby, Tenby and the Fife fishing villages have escaped the ravages of prosperity. This may have been for some perfectly simple reason, like having an uncomfortable shingle beach (Deal) instead of a popular sandy one; or it may just be that, like the Western Isles, they remained remote and out of harm's way while more accessible places were developed. Here and there, at Dunstanburgh, Castle Sinclair and Cuckmere Haven for instance, delightful places are still relatively quiet simply because cars cannot get there: to reach them involves walking a mile or two. Many harbours seem indestructibly beautiful. There are many splendid stucco-terraced sea-fronts (Hove, Brighton, Dover); some fine remaining piers (Llandudno's is the best); and even a single surviving paddle-steamer plying irregularly here and there on pleasure trips on the south coast. And there are still lots of places where you can get donkey rides, see Punch and Judy, and buy fresh fish from, or at least from near, a real fishing boat.

As a boy of eight or nine I used at first to feel a bit strange and shy arriving on an unfamiliar beach. I know why now: no one on a beach escapes scrutiny, everyone is interesting and everyone else has time to look. On the beach humanity spreads itself out in full view, as if on display. Everyone is equally spectator and participant in the relentless process of life. Even the various encumbrances – spades, buckets, balls, beach bags, thermos flasks, towels, nylon windbreaks – seem to suggest the things we casually accumulate throughout life. One sees babies strapped to a parent's chest, children too young to realize they are naked, older ones full of curiosity and energy; boy- and girl-friends, young couples, family groups; the easy-going comfortably middle-aged, the grey-haired but resolutely youthful; the elderly and serene, the old and failing being helped along. People's lives are mostly spent hidden away within four walls, but on the beach people are as unprotected as on a stage; and, if it's hot, almost as naked as when they were born.

In these respects the seaside scene remains much as it always was. However much clothes and belongings change, people on the beach still look pretty much as they did in old photographs. Children and parents, grannies and aunties, virginally white or freshly reddened by the sun and wind, can everywhere be seen enjoying or enduring the public family life of the beach, a place without hassle or dignity, privacy or modesty. People in shopping arcades and at the amusements, on the cliff railway or the beach tramway, energetic in the morning or worn out by tea-time, coping with hunger, thirst, boredom, fractious children or exhausted parents, splashing in the waves or dozing off unselfconsciously in pay-deckchairs to the sound of the band – none of this has changed greatly, or seems in much danger of doing so.

Dunwich beach

A few years ago I visited a small island in the middle of the Pacific. It was beautiful: small black herons waded in the lagoons, frigate birds sailed in the blue sky, coloured fish swam at the edge of the reef, coconut groves shaded its beaches, coral formations rose like sculpture from the sand and out of the clean sea. But being currently a prosperous island, it was rapidly growing squalid. The shore was ringed with cheaply run-up shacks and with wrecked cars, the sand was dotted with beer cans. It seemed ironic that such a paradise should be so careless of its own beauty and well-being; yet a visitor could feel comfortably superior, could feel that we back home in our own longer-civilized country would have taken better care. But after a journey round our own shores I'm no longer so sure. The things that in that unfamiliar and romantic setting seemed outrageous are the very things that, unthinking or helpless, we are now letting happen to our own coastline. For Britain too is ringed not only by firm sand and sparkling waves, by lovely rocks and clear pools, but by creeping suburbia and the ruins of industry, by car parks and power-stations, by dirty waste dumps and noxious refuse. On the beaches, eager children looking for pebbles, seaweed and shells find instead clusters of polystyrene foam, lumps of black oil, weathered condoms and sandy little balls of excrement.

It is tempting to look at the coatline purely as a spectacle, to consider it with the detachment of an outsider. But it is impossible to be entirely detached; human and social considerations keep intruding. People provide its liveliest aspects and human energy has transformed it. Even its more dismal aspects arise mainly from people's natural desires – to make a living or simply to enjoy the place, whatever overcrowding and mess may follow. So it's no use wishing that the coast could somehow stay unspoilt. For one thing, it's a bit late; for another, it's not so easy to define 'spoilt'. By whom? For whom? 'Spoilt' has a selfish ring; it mostly means merely used by too many other people. The shoreline was the first place to make its living out of being beautiful; ironically, for sooner or later this activity becomes self-defeating. Commercial pressures have always been at work shaping and transforming the coast, but it is no longer reasonable to believe that market forces can be trusted to work to the general good. Mostly they do not; in a consumer society it is in the end the environment that gets consumed. So the prospects for the coastline today are poor; for three reasons. First, our technical and economic ability to harm the environment is growing; secondly, our attempts to curb this ability are ineffective and out of favour politically; and thirdly, there is less and less environment left.

To accept this state of affairs would be short-sighted anywhere, but to do so in this country is also bad business. England invented the seaside. It was at Scarborough, Weymouth, Sidmouth, Brighton that people first learnt how to market the attractions of the seashore. Indeed, much of the delight of the seaside is due to a conscious and skilful balance between its exploitation and its preservation. It was also in this country that the first organization was set up to safeguard the environment: if it were not for the National Trust, many of the most beautiful stretches of the coast would long ago have succumbed to the unchecked and uncontrollable forces of the enterprise culture. But now, as the country begins reluctantly to realize and accept its reduced significance in the world, tourism is becoming very valuable to us. Indeed, once the oil has gone, it looks as if 'Heritage' will be the only thing Britain will have left to sell. Inevitably therefore our landscape and environment are coming to be seen – whether we like it or not – as marketable commodities. But they too are once-only assets – and if, like the oil, they are squandered, we will have nothing left to fall back on.

The seashore, however, is much too interesting a place for anyone there to care to dwell for long on the follies of the present or the grisliness of future prospects. It is also too mysterious. Newton wrote, 'I seemed only a boy playing on the seashore, and diverting myself in now and then finding a smoother pebble or a prettier shell than ordinary, whilst the great ocean of truth lay all undiscovered before me.' The sea represents the permanent, the inaccessible, the undiscovered; the beach the place, where the familiar and known things merge into the unpredictable and unfathomable: a place to dip your toe in gingerly or to take a plunge. At the water's edge the ordinary and the commonplace continually melt into the uncertain yet inevitable enigma of the future.

Camden Town, February 1988

The East coast

By and large the east is empty. The typical East Anglian seashore is an expanse of sand or shingle overlooked by an unbroken line of wooden beach huts, flimsy in appearance but durable, a shelter against the rawness of the elements and a social fortress against unwelcome intruders. Behind all this lies a quiet town, of flint, red and grey brickwork and white paint, with an occasional Dutch gable imported from just across the water, and some open green spaces with ancient cannon beside a coastguard station. The smells are of malt and the familiar, pleasantly rotten scent of the shore; the sounds are of terns, shelduck and, except on Sundays, of the USAF's tank-busters from Bentwaters; the light is from a grey sky broken by sparkling but patchy shafts of sunshine. The shore stretches on beyond the town until it is backed only by reed-fringed marshland, a desolate landscape whose skyline is marked by distant church towers, by white-cowled brick maltings, and by the big grey concrete cube of a nuclear power-station or the pipes and flare-stacks of an offshore gas terminal. Out to sea are a few small fishing boats and the ungainly silhouettes of some idle oil-rigs crouching like Bosch monsters. Minsmere, Blakeney Point, Scolt Head are such wild and empty places; indeed, the southern shore of the Wash near Gedney Drove End, with its red-and-white-striped target ships out on the mud, is the bleakest and most featureless tract in the country.

Until recently, inaccessibility, and not being on the way to anywhere in particular, protected the East Anglian coast from the havoc wrought elsewhere by prosperity, market forces and the fast buck. Laissez-faire, better roads and faster trains are changing this. The region's traditionally depressed reputation as the salesman's graveyard, though now inaccurate, has preserved its beauty for the visitor.

Southwold

To the inhabitants it no doubt seems forlorn, a place which hasn't properly caught up, whose traditional commercial strengths have weakened. To the artist, conscious of its billowy light-filled skies and its distant level horizons, it is magnificent.

On its 'bracing' shingle or sand beaches, the only shelter is from the groynes put there to stop the shore inching away. Because of the flatness the beaches are often backed by areas of marsh and broadland well below sea level. There are long, wide estuaries, once full of oysters, eels, dabs and ducks; the local boats were the low, flat duck-punts of the wildfowlers. East Anglian ports used to be prosperous, and a few like Mistley, Lowestoft and Boston remain flourishing. Some, like Dunwich, have been almost entirely washed away; others, like Ipswich, have shrivelled and changed as their trade in timber and corn dwindled, or have adapted like Felixstowe, Yarmouth and King's Lynn, as container, freezer or offshore oilfield supply ports. The once characteristic scenery of timber yards, Thames barges, fishing quays and brick maltings has changed to meet the needs of containers and the whims of commuters. Holiday-makers are putting down roots. Indeed, the first seventy-five miles or so out of London is now almost all thin suburbia. Further on there are oases of solid comfort and modest prosperity in Frinton, Aldeburgh, Southwold, Cromer. North of Great Yarmouth and again north of the Wash there are tackier areas where caravans, chalets and holiday camps are spread about among the grass of the dunes. This is especially true in Lincolnshire where the coast is closest to the once industrial East Midlands, for which Skegness and Mablethorpe are as handy as Blackpool is for Manchester and Lancashire and the north-west.

Mersea Island and the Strood Channel

The first Essex landscapes I got to know really well, by drawing
them repeatedly in all kinds of weather and tides and by sailing
over them, were the mudflats of the Stour at Mistley. The interest
was two-fold – the ever-changing light as patches of sunlight and
cloud shadows drifted across the featureless mud, and the ebb or
flow of the tide, filling as it flowed first the deep and winding
channel and then its smaller tributary creeks, and gradually
engulfing even the remaining plateaux and hummocks of the mud
banks. In the end you could no longer tell whether you were
looking at thin, almost liquid, mud or at the shallow but
unbroken sea that now stretched right across your field of vision.
Apart from swans and shelduck, the only moving things in the
landscape were wading birds, never near enough for me to identify
but visible even from far away as a dense little cloud moving fast
over the water and all at once darkening as the birds turned and
dropped on to the mud. This drawing is of the Strood Channel
which separates Mersea Island on the left from the flat Essex
mainland, looking down towards the mouth of the Blackwater.

mersea Island and the Strood Channel

Southend, Walton and Mistley

The Southend waterfront is cheerful, vulgar, raucous and cosmopolitan. Such homely or native-sounding amenities as Peter Pan's Playground are now outshone by the lights of Las Vegas Amusements and the Las Vegas Grill (chicken–pies–fish and chips–scampi–takeaway bar). Royal Terrace, where Nelson stayed, is a hotch-potch, each house differently detailed, sometimes brick, sometimes stucco; but every house has a balcony, which gives an overall impression of unity and delight, a reminder of Southend's distinguished place in the development of English seaside architecture.

Walton, which began a few decades later than Southend, about 1830, lacks the splendour but the raucousness is safely concentrated and bottled up inside a big hangar on the pier. The beach huts are the unmistakable sign of a family resort. Six miles down the coast, beyond polite and genteel Frinton, Clacton pumps 4,000,000 tons of sewage sludge a year into the North Sea.

Mistley Quay is one of the most magical places I know. Thirty years ago I painted a series of watercolours of its cliff-like maltings; and the same year I learned how to sail a dinghy up and down this stretch of brown water, during the four or five hours of high water when it turned from a landscape of smelly mud into a fresh, occasionally fierce sea. It is still a curiously timeless place. The twin towers of Adam's church, and the stone swan in its pond, are all that remain of Mistley as a spa. Who would have wanted to come all this way to spend half the day looking at mud? But the port itself, which seemed terminally sleepy when I used to draw there in the fifties, has revived, with a flourishing trade in timber and grain. The channel is dredged now, and there is new gear for unloading the timber. But the sweet smell of malt fills the air, and the old maltings, though now timber offices and minus their old cowls, are still magnificent in scale, the bricks green with lichen, a pair of kestrels purring up in the high gables.

Mistley Quay

17

Ipswich and Felixstowe

Like Mistley, many East Anglian seaport quays are quite far from the open sea, up estuaries and even rivers. Tilbury on the Thames, Maldon on the Blackwater, Colchester on the Colne, Ipswich on the Orwell are only the first of many. And in Constable's time seagoing boats went far higher up the Stour than Mistley, to Bergholt and Nayland and even up to Sudbury; it was easier than lugging their cargoes about on land. Now of course there's no point. Inland quayside warehouses have had to find other uses and their hoists and gantries have become evocative left-overs.

But some ports have kept going, adapting to new purposes or merely – like Ipswich – renewing and extending their old roles as timber and grain ports with the flour mills conveniently at hand. There is an interesting mixture of building materials on the quayside buildings – the naked concrete and the painted corrugated iron just as much as the red brick, wood and stone of the older warehouse and the splendid Old Custom House of 1845. I like the way that, at Ipswich, layer after layer of solid building has risen behind the original waterside skyline, overlaying it but adding something real and practical.

Warehouse at Battlesbridge

Ipswich dock and the Old Custom House

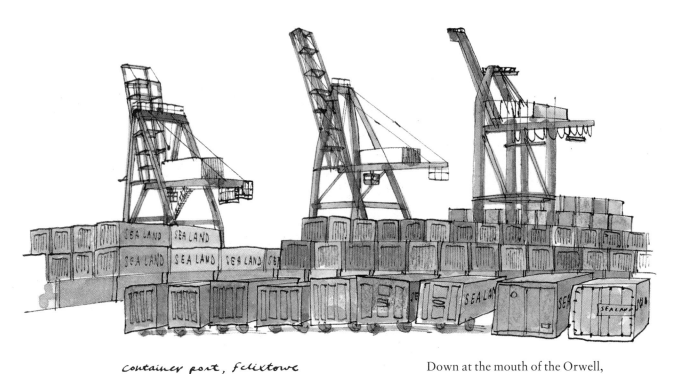

container port, Felixstowe

Down at the mouth of the Orwell, Felixstowe is an example of the newer kind of port with no call for any quayside buildings at all: the goods it handles carry their own protective casing round with them and the administrative portacabins look hardly more substantial than the containers. There is no point in building monumental dockyard walls when a bit of wire netting keeps people out just as effectively and far more cheaply. The distinctive container-port cranes, looking like giant horses, face the riverside docks, turning their backs on the other seafront aspect of Felixstowe, whose skyline they dominate none the less. Just over the river in Harwich is a bizarre reminder of the prison hulks of Victorian days: a disused roll-on/roll-off car ferry, the M V *Earl William*, housing detained immigrants, with table tennis and badminton where the car decks used to be.

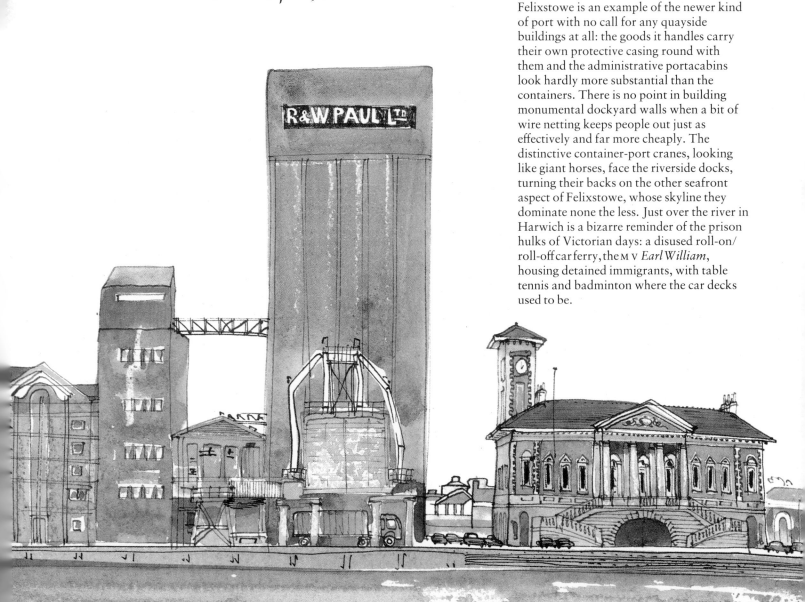

Aldeburgh

Aldeburgh, Sizewell and Minsmere

I knew Britten's *Sea Interludes* long before I saw Aldeburgh; ever since, the shingle and the boats, the waves and the terns have seemed inseparable from the music. On a summer Sunday morning, though, the pretty candy-coloured seafront is sweeter and more comfortable than the Borough of Peter Grimes can have been. 'Music Weekly' drifts out of the open windows and people come out to read the Sunday papers in the sunshine: boats putt-putt lazily in towards the shingle with their catch, the life-boat opens up for visitors and big fibreglass ice-cream cones appear by the Moot Hall.

On these steep shingle beaches the boats are winched up beyond the high-water mark. The diesel winch engines are such a familiar and unchanging feature of the shore that you hardly notice them. Everything looks haphazard but all the bric-à-brac has a function – the heavy driftwood planks are to ease the boat's way over the shingle, the rusty old cables are sturdier than they seem and well able to haul the boat up the beach, the unwanted bits of greasy scrap-metal left lying around are really turntables for the keels. The only changes discernible in the seashore gear over thirty years or so are that the boats have radios and that the old wooden fish boxes have mostly been replaced by bright plastic ones; the fishermen's buoys and marker pennants are of plastic too.

Sizewell beach

At Sizewell the shore scene is identical; only the background has
changed. The big concrete slabs of Sizewell A dominate the
horizon from either direction. There is a fine view of them beyond
the Minsmere marshes from the National Trust car park at
Dunwich Heath. From here you can walk down through the
brambles, along the grassy bank beside the Minsmere bird
sanctuary, and then return along the wave-patterned shingle.

Minsmere

Dunwich, Blythburgh and Southwold

I first heard of Dunwich at school, mentioned with disapproval as the remnant of a once prosperous Saxon and Norman port which still sent members to Parliament long after all its buildings had crumbled away into the sea. The remains of its sandy cliff can be seen, still crumbling. But the harbour vanished when the river was diverted up the coast into the marshes towards Walberswick; the site is now a car park, with a café and an open-air fish shop just behind the shingle fishing beach with its small collection of boats. It is usually windy here and you need to keep moving, down the beach towards Dunwich Heath and Minsmere or up towards the beautiful marshes. This stretch of the east coast is the bit with the most character, often bleak and raw but always fresh and invigorating. Blythburgh too used to be a port with a busy quayside near its fine church. Where the Blyth estuary widens you can still see the timber-strengthened banks of the original channel.

Southwold is the perfect east-coast town. You can walk along the pretty front at three levels – down on the beach, on the concrete esplanade, or up above the black huts along the lanes and paths behind the white railings. There is a white lighthouse positioned well back from the shore, and a pretty grass-covered vantage point called Gun Hill with a row of *c.*1600 cannon pointing out at Sole Bay to ward off privateers. One summer when my children were small a friend let us use one of the wooden beach huts and we instantly found out how useful it was as a base and a refuge. Because the huts look so much alike, they need names: Bay View, Spindrift, Nineteen, Billy Bumpkin, Try Again, Siesta or Sweet Martini. Just to the left of the top picture is the Sailors' Reading Room of 1864, a big quiet room with model fishing boats, figureheads, and good pictures of weather-beaten Southwold sailors.

Gun Hill, Southwold

Southwold

23

Hemsby

24 Cromer

Hemsby and Cromer

When I was seven we had a fortnight's holiday near Great Yarmouth, where I saw the big fleet of herring drifters and first tasted the delicious bloaters. My parents had rented one of the wooden bungalows – I don't think they can have been called chalets at that time – on the hummocky dunes. One day my father painted a watercolour of the view from it: of a wooden gate and fencing and wire-netting stuck in the grassy sand, with, further away, the heavy grey sky and the sea luminous and greenish beneath it. Hemsby beach was very exposed; I flew a kite, and can remember the sharp stinging sensation on my ankles as the dry sand was whipped low along the beach by the bitter wind. A steady procession of small fishing boats and coasters passed to and fro in front of us, heading in and out of Yarmouth.

Our friends on the beach were a brother and sister from Doncaster, a bit older; their father was a miner. They had taken the bus in to Yarmouth one day for an outing but hadn't liked it much, as the parents had quarrelled all the time. The summer evenings were long and light, but my mother thought that children needed 'a good night's rest' and my brother and I were put to bed ridiculously early, in broad daylight. As we lay obediently tucked up reading Hans Andersen at ground level in our bungalow, and therefore in full view, we were laughed at by the streams of children passing to and fro along the dunes path, their day still in full swing. The bungalow was just behind the ones slipping down the dunes in this picture. There is a big field full of caravans there now, and further back still are terraces of holiday homes and the Golden Nugget Prize Bingo amusements shop. The beach has ice-cream vans and a beach rescue vehicle; the small boats have disappeared but a succession of red helicopters passes overhead between Yarmouth and the oil-rigs.

Cromer, like nearby Sheringham, is altogether grander, with a tall church, hotels, a delicate cast-iron pier and a fleet of crab boats. Above the fishing beach is a garden with a model village which includes a lighthouse, a well-observed thirties – modern cinema, Sandringham, and a pair of Norfolk cottages cunningly thatched with old doormats.

Blakeney Channel

Blakeney, Hunstanton, The Wash and Huttoft Bank

The most isolated part of the coast is the long, thin shingle beach of Blakeney Point. As you plod along the shingle it is quite featureless apart from the scalloped patterns of the foam from the breaking waves. On the inland side of the dyke is Blakeney Channel, full of dinghies and edged by grassy banks with good walking paths.

Everything is horizontal. Along the coast at Hunstanton even the cliffs are flat like a layer-cake made of red sandstone with a thick icing of white chalk, a red chalk filling in between and plenty of broken off icing lying at the bottom. The effect is surprising: it looks diagrammatic and artificial. There are more red-and-white stripes along the southern edge of The Wash, where painted target ships for bombing practice are the only visible features in a landscape otherwise completely empty through 180 degrees. I had been looking forward to a view of The Wash, but when you have followed the narrowing concrete roads across the level farmland to where they peter out, there is nothing to see but this olive-green wilderness. After such a desert, the beach at Huttoft Bank near Mablethorpe with its orderly groynes seems positively overcrowded with features.

The Wash at Gedney Drove End

Cliffs at Hunstanton

Huttoft Bank

King's Lynn and Boston

King's Lynn at the southerly tip of The Wash and Boston at the westerly are substantial and historic towns, their past commercial importance and maritime activities still reflected in their fine brick and stone buildings, even where these have lost their old significance. For both towns have seen better days. Boston was once the most important port in the country, though it is hard to believe this today when, looking down into the River Witham, you can see only thin sections of its splendid riverside buildings reflected between the expanses of mud. It is only when you climb Boston Stump, the great tower of its parish church, and can see the river winding away to the Victorian docks that you realize how close the sea is. But in the town, the riverside now has a ravaged air – some ample and beautiful warehouses are left standing, partly restored and partly derelict, but they are surrounded by curious and pointless-looking open spaces on which stand old overgrown boats and parked cars.

On the other hand, there is nothing mysterious about the sea's link with King's Lynn. From the quayside the Ouse shoots out, straight as an arrow, to The Wash, as if between ruled banks. The town's prettiest structure is the 1683 Custom House, which now stands by a dock just as muddy as Boston's. This Wren-style building is now dwarfed, but not spoilt, by tall grain elevators made of painted concrete. Ships would never have found their way into Lynn, through the tortuous channels and hard sandbanks of The Wash, without pilots. A suitably elegant and distinguished Pilot's Office stands on the end of the quay, its octagonal tower affording good views up and down the river. The other Royal seaside towns, Lyme Regis and Bognor Regis, received their Royal status as rewards for services rendered (Lyme as a base for Edward I against the French, in 1284; Bognor for having cured George V after an illness in 1928). But Lynn used until 1537 to be Bishop's Lynn until Henry VIII appropriated it.

The River Witham at Boston

Boston

King's Lynn

King's Lynn

Boston Stump

Custom House, King's Lynn

King's Lynn

North East England

North of the Humber the east coast gets bleaker and wilder. The big fishing ports fish less or not at all nowadays and their quays are emptier. The loneliest region of all is the low flat land of Holderness, its ragged sky scratched and pricked by church spires, chemical works and gas terminals. Then as you go further north the coast gets bonier and more dramatic: Flamborough Head has the best stretch of chalk cliffs after Sussex, though they are curiously different in form from those on the south coast, jigsaw shapes instead of straight and clean-cut edges. The towns and villages are fewer, smaller, more isolated, and made of stone instead of brick or Norfolk flint. The long narrow fishing boats or 'cobles' are built on Viking lines.

It is more industrial than East Anglia. Unmistakable traces of the early chemical industry, though softened by time and overgrown, still mark the tall alum-bearing cliffs at Hummersea Scar near Staithes. From here on, the coastal views from the bleak little resorts begin to include iron- and steelworks, blast furnaces and retorts – advance warnings of an industry that comes to the boil around Middlesbrough, flaming, hissing and erupting into the clogged and poisoned air. Silence and tranquillity return as one approaches the empty, hushed shipyards of Hartlepool, Sunderland and Tyneside proper. Everything here seems poorer and idler than anything does further south: the government money meant to reinvigorate the area seems to have melted away into inhuman hardware and mechanical processes rather than into activities in which people can play any visible part. So the jobless men scavenge the beaches for coal, or wander in autumn along the clifftops past the pigeon lofts, looking for blackberries. In the sun it looks, as a way of life, quite enviable. There is an air of patient, resigned and almost compliant purposelessness, of filling-in time – of classic industrial depression.

The north-east coast has several splendid towns. Scarborough is the most sedate and elegant of all the northern resorts, with a castle, a fine Bath-type crescent, and long sea-fronts on two different bays. The lofty and staid residential town is connected with the lively harbour and beach by shady woodland gardens. But I like Whitby even better, for its less pretentious style, for its double piers shaped like a pair of tongs or calipers, and for the magnificent ruins of its clifftop abbey.

There are beautiful villages too. My favourite is Staithes, its austere little harbour enclosed by rough brown cliffs, its small fishing fleet still putting out to sea early in the dawn light. Some villages, like Robin Hood's Bay, though very pretty, have become too touristy for comfort; others, like Seahouses and Beadnell, still have fascinating working harbours, whose fine quayside lime-kilns have the same solidity and structural perfection as the great northern castles. Seashore industries have become bigger but less elegant since those kilns were built. But here and there are curious left-overs, like the upturned boats on the shore at Holy Island: weather-beaten and shabby, but a reminder of a straightforward time when willingness to work secured for any able northerner the opportunity to do so.

The emptiness of the north-east is not so much a sign of the troubled present as a permanent state: it was there always. On the headlands stand, not only giant power-stations and smelters, but smaller landmarks: ruined castles and abbeys like Bamburgh, Dunstanburgh, Lindisfarne. Out to sea, as well as the fleets of disused tankers riding at anchor, you see the low flat shapes of the bare Farne Islands. Like the empty shipyards, the castles and abbeys are dramatic reminders, but of a more distant past, its significance and its relevance to our own lives now hard to remember or even to imagine. The untouched serenity of certain parts is striking but temporary: the wild dunes and empty beaches of Druridge Bay, perhaps the finest stretch of coastline left in the north-east, have been earmarked as the site for a nuclear power-station.

harbour, Staithes

Spurn Head

Spurn Head is extremely odd: a thin sliver of land three and a half
miles long but sometimes only fifty yards wide, which hangs down
across the mouth of the Humber. You can drive down it to the big
black-and-white lighthouse. Here and there on the way you can
see the sandy North Sea on the one hand and the muddy estuary
on the other and feel you could easily lob a stone into either. I saw
it on a grey hazy day early in October. A mile or two out to sea
were tankers waiting for the tide so that the Humber pilots could
board them and guide them up to the refineries and chemical
works at Paull on the outskirts of Hull. The road down the spit
has a military flavour, with disused railway lines crisscrossing it or
running alongside and various ruined remains of defence works:
broken concrete and rusty stakes at the high-water mark on the
estuary side, and solid concrete and lines of battered wooden
piling, as if of a silted-up jetty, on the beach. In autumn all the
birds migrating south down the coast are funnelled wing-tip
to wing-tip into this narrow strip. So are all the bird watchers.

The beach at Spurn Head

33

Flamborough Head

I wasn't really expecting to find any chalk in the north-east, supposing it to be pretty well confined to the south coast, so Flamborough Head was a surprise. Its scale and splendour are impressive, and the sea has weathered and worn the cliff edge into a curious and intricate shape. Walking round it, you feel like an ant crawling round a piece of jigsaw-puzzle. Down in the small coves are several rock-stacks, one so fragile-looking that you feel it ought to have toppled over long ago. An equally fragile yet durable structure stands a little back from the sea on the high ground at the centre of Flamborough Head: the tower of the Old Beacon, an elegant octagon of chalk and darker stone in four stages, still a striking landmark. The current lighthouse, nearer the sea, is also white, but much more familiar in form. The only other lighthouse colours are red and black: an example is the manned Longstone Lighthouse further up the coast on the Farne Islands, a sharp touch of colour in a blue-grey-green landscape. The automatic lighthouse on Inner Farne is black-and-white like the island's seabirds. Most lighthouses, enjoying isolated positions and being simply designed, geometrical in form and simply or even childishly painted, are as satisfyingly perfect as well-turned chess pieces or pepper-pots. But the most ambitious and most elegant lighthouse I know is the one on the West Pier at Whitby: a finely modelled Doric column on a solid cube of stone, perfect in its fluting and entasis, supporting a square platform and a pretty octagonal domed lantern with a weathervane. It upstages everything else in sight, making the white wooden capstans on the pier look like Daleks and the red and green harbour lights – really very handsome in their own right – look like candles stuck in painted barrels.

Rock stack, Flamborough Head

Old beacon tower, flamborough Head

Spurn Head

Whitby

Farne Islands

Farne Islands

Flamborough Head

37

Filey: Primrose Valley and Butlin's

The road into Filey winds steeply down through a tunnel of woodland and emerges virtually on the beach. There is a yellow-brick lifeboat shed, the boat hiding inside. On the slipway stand Yorkshire cobles, fat-bellied, their lines sagging and ungainly when dragged out of the water on their trolleys. Their nets are hung over the railings like towels on a towel-rail. The pub has a 'family room' and the shop sells fishing nets, beach balls and dual-control super stunt kites with jumbo twenty-five-foot tails. There is a little grey hut for the parking attendant and two severe notice boards forbidding vehicles on the beach and cautioning boat users. On the right there is an esplanade curving away into the roke (local patois for seamist); on the left a headland and Filey Brigg, an offshore reef.

On the cliffs above is Primrose Valley: a greenfield caravan site spaciously laid out round a central fun area. On the wide roads a tractor-drawn train carries you on a circular route taking in Reception, Hire Goods, Shops, Cafeteria, Toilets, Sportsfield,

Primrose Palace, Tavern and Theatre Bars, and various other bars and chalet areas. Here I met a retired Grimsby skipper who had bought one of the big caravans – a Vogue 30 perhaps, or a Riviera Monaco, or an Executive – off the peg at the site a few years ago. 'Van' owners plant and maintain their own immediate surroundings, the management the rest, so the place is far easier and cheaper to run than the old holiday camp had been, with all its expensive redcoats. The old Butlin's lay abandoned and desolate-looking next door, inside a tough steel fence. Though at first glance it looked a bit sinister, it also looked touching: plenty of its young holidaymakers must have become grandparents long ago. But Primrose Valley looked for the time being at least quite splendid, with the sun coming out, lots of roses and white-painted chain fencing, flower borders and a trim lawn round each vehicle, more flowers in white urns at the front doorsteps, screens of rosebushes round the big rubbish bins, the distant Yorkshire hillsides and the grey sea down below.

Abandoned holiday camp, Filey

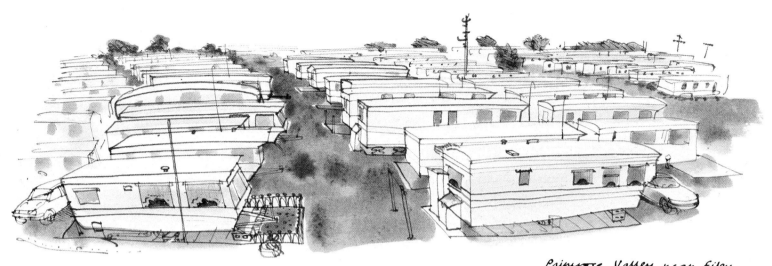

Primrose Valley near Filey

Whitby

My son, who was seven or eight at the time, came with me on some of the journeys of exploration I made for this book and had rides on most of these things. He loved them all: even the Traum Boot which left me feeling uncomfortably battered afterwards. But I can't help feeling he was getting short measure all the same, for most of them are ugly and shoddily designed.

When I was a student, people were just getting interested in 'the English popular tradition': especially in Victorian pubs and fairgrounds with all the exuberant and skilful decoration of their steam organs, proudly striding cockerels and galloping horses. They were bright and vulgar and beautifully done, and they are now cherished as valuable antiques. The stuff my son rides on, if it's fibreglass, is derived either from comic strips or from military hardware; if it's heavy-duty inflatable it's formula-designed, off a production line. Luckily, there are still plenty of places where a child can get a ride on a real donkey.

The Yorkshire resort with the most distinct character is Whitby. It is cut in two by the River Esk which flows out between two fine symmetrical piers. High on a cliff on the quieter eastern side stand the ruins of Whitby Abbey and the churchyard of St Mary's, whose voluptuous and swirling gravestones themselves look like the choppy grey-brown waves below.

Staithes and Hummersea Scar

Staithes is a huddle of stone buildings
tumbling down a hillside into Staithes Beck.
I stayed in an ancient-looking quayside
house facing the breakwater and the
slipway, green with slippery weed, and
woke to see a few fishing cobles putting out
into a quiet sea: all that remain of the
hundred-strong fleet of Edwardian times.

Three miles up the coast at Hummersea
Scar, a tall cliff has at some distant time
been half eaten away by the mining of alum.
Although it all looks quiet and overgrown
now, this was Britain's earliest chemical
industry. The coastline about here forms
part of the North Yorks Moors national
park, which has been designated as
geologically suitable for the dumping of
radioactive waste. But for the present this
is still a lovely place to walk, with springy
turf, grass yellowing as it dries, and thickets
of bramble.

42

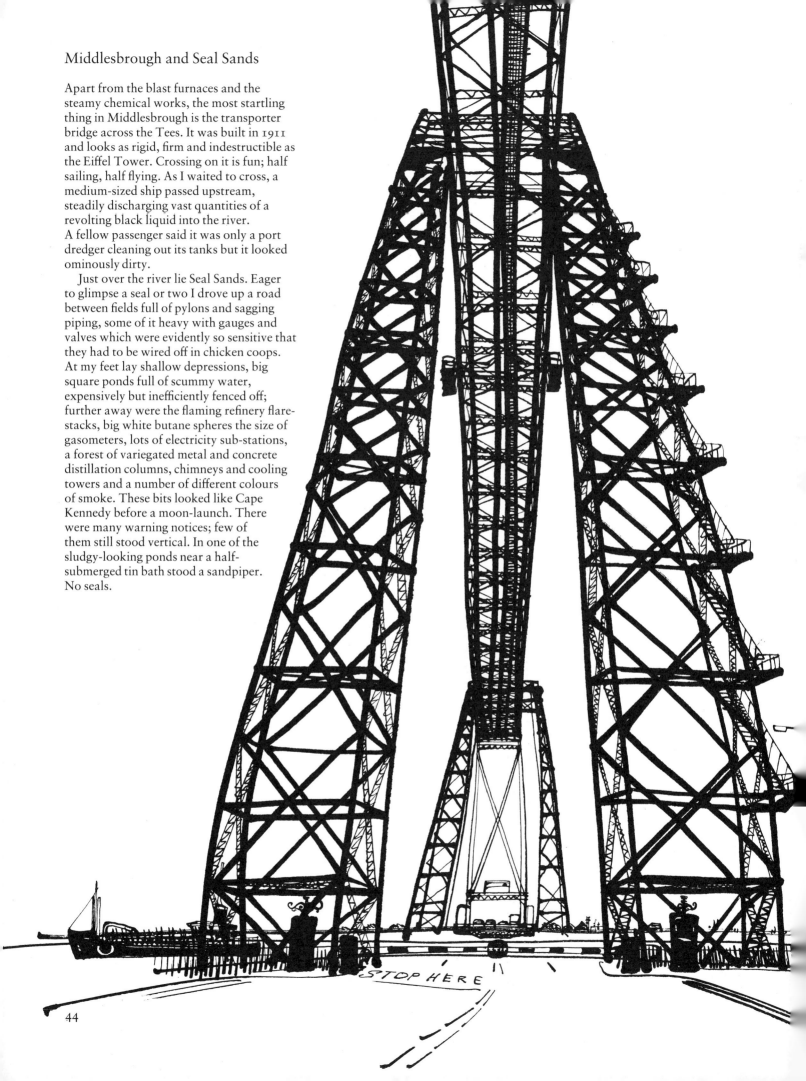

Middlesbrough and Seal Sands

Apart from the blast furnaces and the
steamy chemical works, the most startling
thing in Middlesbrough is the transporter
bridge across the Tees. It was built in 1911
and looks as rigid, firm and indestructible as
the Eiffel Tower. Crossing on it is fun; half
sailing, half flying. As I waited to cross, a
medium-sized ship passed upstream,
steadily discharging vast quantities of a
revolting black liquid into the river.
A fellow passenger said it was only a port
dredger cleaning out its tanks but it looked
ominously dirty.

Just over the river lie Seal Sands. Eager
to glimpse a seal or two I drove up a road
between fields full of pylons and sagging
piping, some of it heavy with gauges and
valves which were evidently so sensitive that
they had to be wired off in chicken coops.
At my feet lay shallow depressions, big
square ponds full of scummy water,
expensively but inefficiently fenced off;
further away were the flaming refinery flare-
stacks, big white butane spheres the size of
gasometers, lots of electricity sub-stations,
a forest of variegated metal and concrete
distillation columns, chimneys and cooling
towers and a number of different colours
of smoke. These bits looked like Cape
Kennedy before a moon-launch. There
were many warning notices; few of
them still stood vertical. In one of the
sludgy-looking ponds near a half-
submerged tin bath stood a sandpiper.
No seals.

STOP HERE

44

NIL DESPERANDUM

X AUSPICE DEO X

46

Sunderland from the Bridge

Hartlepool, Sunderland and Wallsend

The shipyards of the north-east were – for an island dependent on trading – surprisingly empty. In a shipyard, the hardest thing to conceal is inactivity; it stares you in the face and shouts. In Hartlepool, Sunderland and on Tyneside I saw plenty of impressive and interesting shipbuilding equipment, but the only work visibly under way in Hartlepool was the restoration of HMS *Warrior*, the first-ever ironclad battleship (now at Portsmouth). Sunderland, despite the Latin tag on the bridge, has turned from shipbuilding to flag-of-convenience car-assembly work for the Japanese. And the only ship I could see being built in Wallsend was the replacement for one of the warships sunk in the Falklands; nothing, in short, of much apparent relevance to this island's present-day commercial needs. I made a careful but fruitless search for the streets I'd seen on an earlier visit: narrow alleys, back-to-back, with roughly hewn stone setts and stone-flagged pavements, flanked by brick walls and the back doors of low terraced houses. Each street then pointed down to big dockyard cranes and the giant hull of a half-built supertanker, so close at hand that it seemed to be standing in the last backyard. Now those streets have vanished as completely as the tankers.

HMS Warrior

Shipyards at Wallsend

Dunstanburgh and Lynemouth

Some of the finest stretches of the north-east coast are in Northumberland. Although Bamburgh is splendid, the most striking of all the northern castles is Dunstanburgh; and as you have to walk the last mile or so you have time to see it taking root and growing in its bleak landscape.

But it no longer looks big or impressive, as it did to Turner, when compared to the power-stations and the aluminium works at Lynemouth. These are fuelled by the collieries that go far out under the sea, and coal waste blackens the shore. Collecting and selling it gives a job to the Cresswell gipsies: you can see them in nippy little carts trotting to and fro like poachers under the official white concrete walls, the NCB railway trucks and the pylons of the power-station. The emptiest and most untouched stretch of all on this coast begins just north of here. Druridge Bay's five miles of wide firm sand is marked only by scattered fronds of seaweed and by the patterns of the wavelets. It is hidden from the land by an unbroken line of dunes. Go and see it quickly before the nuclear power-station is built.

Dunstanburgh Castle

Lynemouth Power Station and Smelter

Quayside at Seahouses

Seahouses and the Farne Islands

Seahouses is a pleasantly ordinary village, with a comfortable hotel, The Olde Ship, a remarkably fine arcade of lime-kilns on the quayside, and an active harbour. From here good solid boats take you out to the Farne Islands – a generally low-lying group of rocks two to four miles out. The skipper gives a commentary. On the voyage out there are grey seals and many seabirds, most memorably the cormorants who stand on the top of the rock stacks, their wings spread out to dry as if on coat-hangers.

From the boat the black rocks seem alarmingly high and slightly theatrical, like ballet scenery. The seals, though alert, look touchingly relaxed and unwary, almost trusting – more like

bathers. Besides the two lighthouses there are one or two isolated buildings – a chapel and a tower – which serve only to emphasize the deserted atmosphere of these strange islands. You can go ashore for an hour or so on Inner Farne to walk round the gently sloping island within a wired-off nature trail. There are a few pools of water among the rock, and greenery a safe distance up from the waves. It was a sunny October morning and the sea was calm; as I returned towards the low flat Northumberland coast, a line of rather plain houses stretching along it in silhouette seemed almost as lonely and dramatic as the grey rock-stacks, the ruins and the lighthouses I had left behind.

The boat to the Farnes

Rock stacks, Staple Island

Old herring boats, Holy Island

Holy Island and Beadnell

The only place where I've ever seen upturned boats made into really substantial, watertight and workmanlike sheds is on the beach at Holy Island. Several of the more interesting of these old herring boats are juxtaposed in the drawing above. When cut in two the boats lose their rigidity and have sagged a bit; they look as if they've come to rely on the tarred sheeting to hold them together. Peggotty's uncle would have looked at home here. The castle on top of the chunk of rock opposite them was rebuilt by Lutyens in 1902 – an astonishing and magically apt conjunction of natural setting and romantic inventiveness, and an example of the most sympathetic aspect of Lutyens' work. Prominent and angular on its hillock, the castle is a solitary dramatic feature in the otherwise unemphatic landscape of the island.

At Beadnell, just south of Seahouses, at the end of a small harbour is an example of an irregularly shaped yet monumental complex of eighteenth-century lime-kilns, a happy product of that indefinable activity in between plain building and formal architecture. The structure comprises arches within arches, winding galleries, mysteriously walled-off recesses and strangely angled courses of stonework at the complex intersection of curved planes. It doesn't appear to face in any particular direction and you can walk round it, through it and over it. Although it doesn't burn lime any longer, at least it is still used for a purpose connected with the sea, the storage of lobster pots. For me it was the most unexpected and unforgettable of the buildings of the north-east coast.

Holy Island

Lime Kilns, Beadnell

Scotland: the East Coast and the North

The coast of eastern Scotland is not renowned for dramatic beauty, and, knowing little of it until recently, I had few preconceptions to be confirmed or dislodged. The appeal of its landscape lies in its detail and its lack of drama, in its freshness and emptiness. Its activities are mostly to do with fish, farming and oil.

North of the border the coast is colder and (except for several big power-stations) almost featureless. Yet where there is activity it is at first glance confident and shrewd, more purposeful than in the north of England. Eyemouth is an active and successful fishing town. The Firth of Forth is spanned by two vast monuments to engineering skill, and a large half-built oil-rig is being completed at Methil on its northern shore. The Fife fishing ports are clean, lively and trim, with an evident self-respect: tourism is not yet calling the tune here, yet I saw no other towns in the country as tempting-looking as these sparkling white and grey and orange towns. Everything on the Fife shore is solid and unpretentious, but substantial. The views from the coastal roads to the blue sea are across good arable farmland entered through solid stone gateways. Life hereabouts looks less profligate than in the south. It's only when one gets to Dundee with its collection of historic ships, its empty dry dock and its deserted quayside warehouses, that things seem to have ground to a halt in the chillingly familiar southern manner: the past cherished and revered, the present left slowly dying. Yet only a bit further on, one is surrounded again by lively going concerns: fishing, curing and shipbuilding in smoky Arbroath and severe Stonehaven, the oil business in the rich, hard and grey northern splendour of Aberdeen with its painted ferries and oil-rig supply boats, its fine granite warehouses and romantically spired skyline.

North of Aberdeen the fishing towns are dour and determined. Their boats look not pretty but coldly efficient, as grey and mean-looking as little warships. Their harbours are vast cruel forests of metal masts, lifting gear and radio aerials. The housing estates look grey and chill; the most memorable views are of power-station and prison (Peterhead) and of gas and oil terminals (St Fergus). But warmth and charm return when the coast turns west towards Inverness and the Moray and Cromarty firths: peaceful inlets, grassy and wooded slopes, well turned out military buildings at Fort George, distillery maltings at Invergordon; pseudo-French-baronial turrets at Dunrobin Castle, bare brochs and ruined sea fortresses like the lonely pair just north of Wick.

On a wet Sunday evening Wick seemed the most dismal town I stayed in on my journey. Yet this far north-eastern corner of Britain has the most haunting coastline. As you approach John o'Groats the landscape slopes away low in the sky and you suddenly begin to be aware of the flat forms of the islands of Orkney, thin and insubstantial in the mist. The rock about here lies in characteristic flat slabs or flags, so that from the high cliffs at Dunnet Head the water's edge looks more like a wet and glistening pavement than a natural shore, and the greeny-grey stone buildings of the region look more like outcrops of rock than carefully laid human shelters.

West of Dounreay with its unearthly nuclear sphere lies only empty coastline with few villages. There are some fine stretches of clean sand but the sense of loneliness intensifies as you drive through a landscape of peat bog and across the Kyle of Tongue to Loch Eriboll. This is a beautiful yet sad place, its shores dotted with the empty and roofless stone walls of dwellings abandoned after the clearances. Despite the dormobiles and the caravans which doss down here and there beside the boulders, and despite the unspoilt sands, this landscape is a fearful and desolate remnant.

fishing fleet, Peterhead

Eyemouth and Tantallon

Eyemouth is hardly five miles into Scotland but is already noticeably Scottish in character – a mixture of traditional village centre, active and prosperous-looking fishing port, and grey housing estate. The boats too are a mixture: some like this with the wheelhouse providing the only shelter, some with a whaleback built forward and sometimes a second covered area amidships to give the fishermen more shelter while they work. Eyemouth fish boxes are still of wood but all the working gear on the boats is metal or plastic, even if like the wheelhouse it is sometimes painted to look like grained wood. Boats and quayside are clean and efficient; the fork-lift truck is Japanese.

   Tantallon Castle looks almost as much a part of the landscape as the rock it is built on, where the Firth of Forth narrows at its mouth: it is, with Dunnottar Castle near Stonehaven, the most spectacularly situated castle on the east coast. The landscape behind the precipitous cliff edges is very flat, which makes the castle look all the more startling. It has the exaggerated scale and the unlikely, almost unbelievable perfection of fairytale castles in old-fashioned children's books or in early romantic water-colours. A mile or two out to sea is Bass Rock, and far beyond it the fishing villages of the Fife coast.

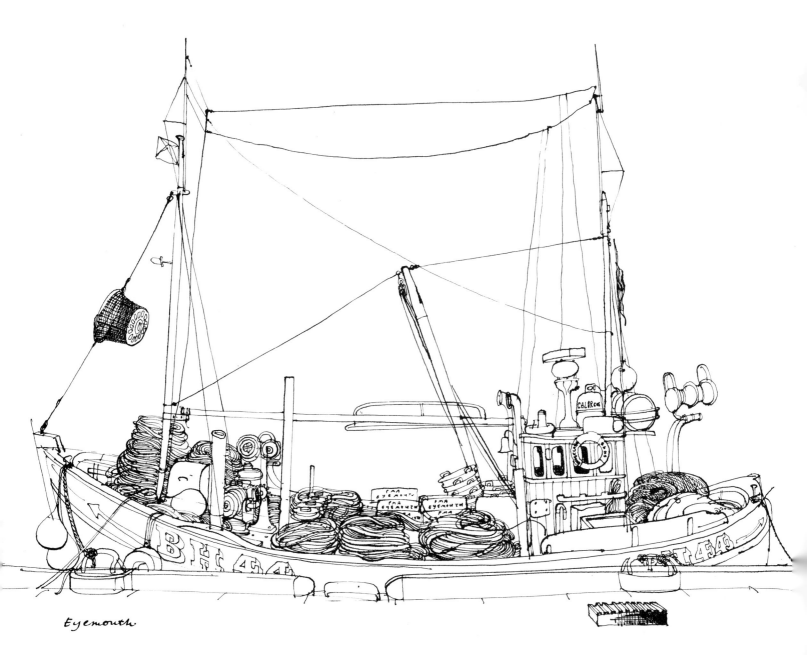

Eyemouth

Tantallon ca

The Forth Rail Bridge

Oil-rig construction at M

The Forth Rail Bridge and Methil

However you see it, glimpsed momentarily over the fields through haze or seen in elevation beyond the newer and much frailer-looking Road Bridge, the Forth Rail Bridge looks astonishing. The scale is unbelievable and the nature of the structure is unfamiliar, unique. Whereas we have become familiar with the enormous yet graceful road-bearing suspension bridges of recent decades – most notably over the Forth, the Severn and the Humber – the vast metal tubes and girders of the three cantilever units of the Forth Rail Bridge look arresting and yet somehow ungainly. There must be tension in the cables of the Road Bridge, but you can't really imagine it for it all looks so effortless, whereas the Rail Bridge makes the task of carrying a railway safely high over this estuary seem arduous, superhuman. The Rail Bridge will by 1990 have served for 100 years. Brunel's smaller Saltash Bridge is another singular structural oddity which has proved just as durable.

Something of the same businesslike ungainliness may be seen across the Forth on the Fife shore in a shipyard at Methil. The oil-rig tower, being built on its side, has the same impressive yet awkward look as a stranded whale or a swan tramping about on dry land. It is a strange sight: the cranes surround it like Macbeth's witches round the cauldron, the ingredients, rusty and still unimpressive, lie around on the ground. Some way out to sea are two other rigs, by now floating and upright. The older Fife towns are famous for their bright colour contrasts: white-washed harling (roughcast) and dark grey stone window surrounds, blue slates or reddish-brown pantiles on the roof. But the housing estates which surround the Methil yard are of uniform drab grey, making the town look like a cement-coloured Welwyn Garden City. Towering over their neat green hedges and monochrome roofs the rig is a colossal intruder. I didn't spot any boatbuilding.

60   The harbour, Crail

Crail

My parents knew and loved the Fife fishing towns and, on their holidays there, painted the views of pantiled roofs seen out of their windows, and the wooden pole frames for the drying nets. I remember as a child often hearing their names being pronounced – Ely, Weems, Saint Monans, Pit and Weem – long before I ever saw them properly spelt on a map: Elie, Wemyss, St Monance, Pittenweem. These towns have had the forethought to look after their appearance and they are still lovely. The rich reddy-browns and concrete greys of the quaysides harmonize well with the pinks and whites and warm stone tints of the houses and, at Pittenweem especially, with the sharp bright fishing-harbour colours: painted boats, bright green plastic nets, luminous red plastic floats. The harbour walls are rough and extremely solid, sometimes of drystone boulder construction. The most attractive harbour wall is the curving, stepped one at Crail. This town is itself two-tiered, with an interesting main street up above its fine harbour. The small pantiled houses are characteristic of Fife: two of those in the drawing are typical in arrangement, with the fishermen's workshop below and the family's quarters above. The other typical local features are the coloured harling, the crow-stepped or corbie gables and the blue and orange roofs.

Dundee, Arbroath, Stonehaven and Dunnottar Castle

Just off Fife Ness, the easternmost tip of Fife, lie the rocks of Carr Briggs. Their old red lightship is now a maritime museum, tied up to a quayside at Anstruther, near Crail. Dundee docks have some fine dockside warehouses, both stone and corrugated-iron; an interesting old dry dock; and a curious assortment of ships – from the historic and well-displayed Unicorn frigate of 1820 to the sturdy oil-rig supply boats now in use, their cargo area aft stripped clear for easy loading. These boats did not seem to my landlubber's eye to be developed from any earlier model but to be a new shape for a new need. On the other hand, the Fraserburgh fishing boat, its working area almost entirely enclosed, looked a clear development from the simpler and prettier toy-like boats of Fife and Arbroath.

Stonehaven is another substantial town of pinky-red stone, with a very fine double harbour. Several of the town's buildings have spires and look from a distance like churches, but are really secular town buildings – a market, a town clock. This kind of municipal local pride, and the spacious square, reminded me of small French towns; it is more typical of Scotland than of England. This harbour smells, not unpleasantly, of fish and diesel oil. It's a nice place in the long summer evening light – people taking their drinks out on the quay, the sounds of conversation

and strolling footsteps, harmless gangs of small boys yelling 'fucking hell' to one another across the water, the piping of oyster-catchers and the sounds of the planes heading for Aberdeen and the late-evening cars starting up. Beyond the harbour are the grassy cliffs on which, a few miles away, stands Dunnottar.

Dunnottar Castle (pp. 64–5), like Tantallon, combines picturesque ruin, remarkable situation and total isolation. Nothing in sight here is in any way incongruous – even the two distant oil-rigs, as lonely on the skyline as planets in orbit, only emphasize the emptiness of the scene; the people who struggle down the steep cliff paths and up the other side to explore the castle seem as much like pilgrims as tourists. It is not easy to say precisely what gives such a scene its attraction, and makes it, however obviously 'pictur-esque', still so interesting to draw. One reason for its appeal is its scale: the size of the rock makes the ruined building look toy-like and harmless and its harsh history seem like a legend. You can see daylight gleaming jewel-like through the empty windows and the rooflessness produces an unusual skyline, jagged and irregular, which engages your curiosity in the same way as a half-built structure does. And the way the walls are shaped to the hummocky rock means that the building seems not merely to stand, but to perch on its base.

The harbour, Stonehaven

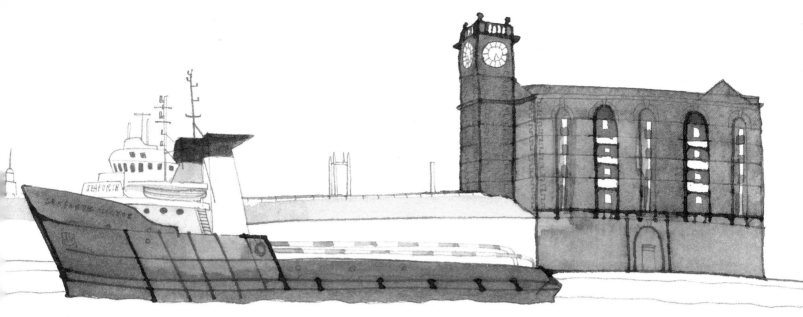

Dundee

NORTH CARR

Anstruther

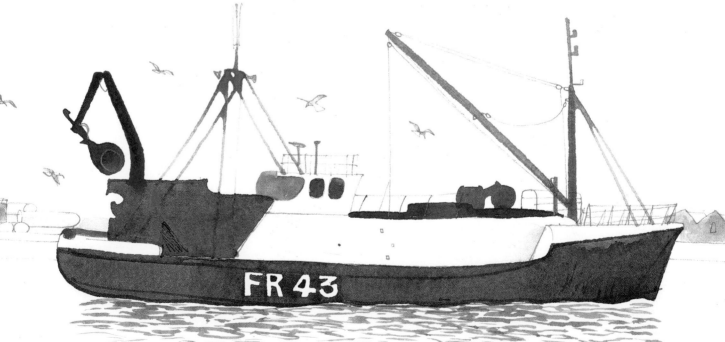

FR 43

Peterhead

64   Dunnottar Castle

Aberdee

Aberdeen to Invergordon

Aberdeen is the greyest city I have ever seen, but it is a bright grey, sparkling and hard as polished granite. Its skyline is as spiked and towered as Edinburgh's, many of its warehouses and offices and public buildings are very fine, and the whole place is oozing self-confidence and oil: indeed, I stepped up to my knee in watery oil in the points of the quayside railway lines. Aberdeen is very big and busy. Further down the coast all you see stacked by the quaysides are plastic fish boxes; here in the smart new offices you see stacked people.

A grey and damp day made Peterhead (p. 54) seem the dourest and harshest place on the coast. But the weather was clearing by the time I reached Fraserburgh, signalled by a funny cast-iron fountain and a pretty harbour. St Fergus was an eighth-century bishop. The village that bears his name is now fired less by burning zeal than by North Sea gas, flaming from the top of the terminal's flare-stacks.

There is an even more traditional or more old-fashioned fishing village than Sandhaven, complete with poles for drying nets, along the coast at Buckie; and Nairn still has its own Fishertown, though the industry itself has ebbed away. Nairn also has a pretty bandstand at the edge of the close-cropped green slopes where Highland Games take place each August.

Fort George was built just after the carnage of Culloden, as a grand and even extravagant gesture in the name of national security; an unnecessary one, in the event, as the threat had already subsided. The walls and turrets of Fort George have that same chilly and menacing precision one sees in present-day military hardware. They could never be picturesque: they look too mean and too efficient for that. On the waterfront at Invergordon may be seen the not wholly dissimilar shapes of the hardware needed to satisfy other human needs: oil for warmth, whisky for contentment.

Sandhaven

St fergus

Buckie

Fraserburgh

Fraserburgh

Nairn

fort george

Invergordon

Lybster and Dunnet Head

North of Inverness the coast is at first deeply indented by the very beautiful Moray, Beauly, Cromarty and Dornoch Firths. After that it straightens out and from then on the sea is never far away from the main road. The August Caithness landscape is agricultural, rich and green, with yellowing cylinders of baled hay in the fields and a few white farmhouses; but you notice that trees and indeed people are getting much thinner on the ground. This feeling is very strong at the almost deserted harbour of Lybster: a smallish yet complex affair with a concrete lighthouse and three separate basins, yet with only a few boats left of the hundred or so it had in early Victorian times. The empty and roofless stone buildings that stand around it were once used for herring curing. The structure of the greeny-black rocks that flank the little cove is remarkable: tossed-about and muddled-looking on the south side but rigidly layered on the north. As you go north, this is the first place where you see the layered rocks, exported in the nineteenth century as flagstones, so characteristic of the country's north-eastern extremity.

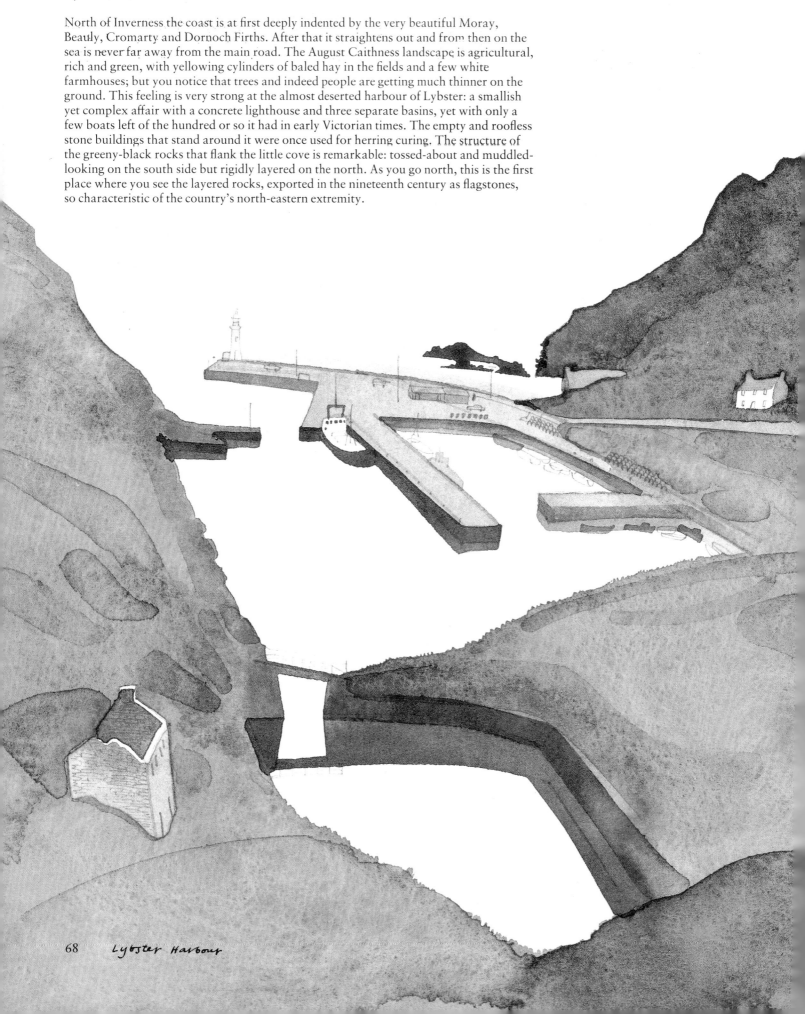

68   *Lybster Harbour*

Duncansby Head near John o'Groats has some magnificent pointed rock stacks. Near its lighthouse is a layby, also used by helicopters, and strewn with wet litter. I prefer the lonely majesty of Dunnet Head, the most northerly tip of the mainland. It too has a lighthouse, yellow-topped and domed. Similarly domed and creamy clusters of hogweed dot the fields and springy turf covers the cliffs, seductively close to the sheer drop down to the flagstones 300 feet below. The views over Orkney are unparalleled and the car park is spotless.

Dunnet Head

Yesnaby and Castle Girnigoe

From the mainland, the Orkney archipelago appears low, flat and tranquil, and its inland landscapes (never in reality more than a few miles from the sea) are gentle and sloping rather than dramatic. But on the western side of the biggest island, Mainland, the coast is fierce and angular, and the layers of rock are not horizontal but curved, swelling and falling away like the swell of the sea. In this lonely part of Britain it is hard to imagine that Orkney has been occupied continually for 6,000 years, for there is nothing in this landscape to suggest the hand of man; only the gentle mewing of the kittiwakes as they wheel about over the swirling rock shapes.

Back in Caithness just north of the dreary town of Wick is the opposite extreme. In an equally lonely setting stand two unearthly monuments to human perseverance, the astonishing cliff-edge ruins of Castle Sinclair and Castle Girnigoe. To reach them at all you have unexpectedly to drive across the runway of a working airfield and then, more appropriately, to walk or wade across a mile of soggy pasture. Most castles are more accessible and much busier. Furthermore, the authenticity of many castles suffers from their being so excessively well maintained – crew-cut lawns and smooth gravel paths, warning notices and safety railings. Such a criticism could hardly be levelled at this pair, which appear completely unrestored. Looking down unprotected at the sea beating the rocks below, you can still feel – as in the fifteenth century – that if you put a foot wrong you're done for.

Fresgoe, Dounreay and Loch Eriboll

The flat Caithness flagstones reappear frequently along the north-facing coast and – wood being scarce – are used as field fencing as well as in the beautiful stonework of the small sandy-bottomed harbour at Fresgoe. Past improvements and additions to the structure can be traced in the way its stones have been laid, a process which has now stopped along with the fishing. But at least one fishing boat remains and a net was drying on a serviceable structure of poles stuck into the quayside grass. Through the harbour entrance can be seen the original sphere and the newer blocks of the reactors of the Dounreay experimental nuclear power-station. This empty region, lacking in potential victims, was a prudent venue for such an undertaking.

West of here the Sutherland coastal landscape is of two kinds – extremely bleak moorland, its monotony broken now and again by sandy bays and inlets and occasionally with pockets of farmland and glimpses of offshore islets. The most noteworthy of the inlets are Kyle of Tongue, crossed by a causeway, and deep Loch Eriboll. Here and there on its eastern side the road follows the pebbly shore, but on the western side you can see the loch only across a barren landscape of bare rock and drystone walls and a few stone buildings. Many of these are no more than ruins; others are enlivened by the cheerful red tints of their rusty corrugated-iron roofs. As subject-matter to draw in a detached way, I like this austere and monochromatic landscape created by the Highland clearances, but in human terms it looks back at you very reproachfully: all sheep, no people. Decent and unremitting endeavour was robbed of its fruits and driven off by powerful, selfish and alien wealth.

At the head of Lock Eriboll rise dramatic mountains which make you realize that the west coast is only round the corner.

Fresgoe Harbour

Loch Eriboll

Scotland: the West Coast

The best-known things about the west of Scotland are not the most intriguing. West coast scenery is famous for being spectacular. But after a day or two one range of mist-shrouded mountains looks very much like another. I'd soon had my fill of empty beaches and rocky promontories, of caravans and passing places, of sheep, of peat bog and picturesque ruins, of magnificence and midges.

But these are the obvious, inescapable things. In its details, the landscape is surprising and fascinating: the unexpectedly springy folds and curves of the rocks, the gaudiness of the lichens, the feathery haze of dry grass between the boulders, the beautiful sombre colours of peat, seaweed and dark stone. I also love the contrasting notes of bright colour on the things man has added to the landscape: yellow oilskins, rust on tin roofs, whitewash on bungalows; coloured paint on lorries, fishing boats and ferryboat funnels. And I like the formal design of the simplest waterside architecture, as at Shieldaig or Ullapool, where only a long white strip of low buildings divides the shore from the hinterland.

West coast assets are white sand and untrodden beaches. There is no sewage and you can see through the water; the space and emptiness are remarkable. The uncertain weather brings dramatic skies which spotlight the landscape, blackening or obscuring the rest. The roads curve and twist round the mountains and along the shores of lochs so that you seldom know which way you are facing or whether an expanse of water is freshwater, loch or sea. From a boat, the coast appears wild and magically remote, its rocks and strands and islets unexplored; everything belongs to the cormorants, the guillemots and the seals. It is easy as a summer visitor to feel only a delightful sense of distance and inaccessibility, as if the landscape were truly left behind and untouched by the ravages of the present day. But development and exploitation are racing ahead nevertheless – marinas, holiday villages, mineral extraction and afforestation, the armed services, fish farming and tourism.

The most spectacular examples of instant industrial archaeology are the relics of the oil-rig construction business which scar some virgin shorelines. At Plockton and on Loch Kishorn, untouched landscapes have been industrialized for oil and then run down again into dereliction within the space of a few years.

The strangest and bleakest places I saw were the islands of South Uist. You reach them from Skye on a cheerfully packed and cosmopolitan car-ferry; but when you disembark, everybody instantly melts away in a puff of car exhaust, absorbed into a vast treeless landscape of peat bog and sea loch. I'd gone there hoping to find some ancient turf-covered cottages, and there indeed they were. Most of them were in a rather sorry state, the roofs looking like neglected and overgrown landscapes. But the characteristic Uist buildings are of more recent origin: small square houses, ground-floor and attic, or plain bungalow, often tin-roofed, plonked down by the road or scattered on an expanse of turf. Everywhere you go the sky reaches down into the landscape, reflected in water that may look like enclosed loch but is really an extension of the sea.

This mingling of land and sea is the region's most beautiful feature. Many places which are as the crow or the light aircraft flies no distance away from the mainland centres are laborious to get to and rewardingly quiet when you arrive. Sea lochs reach right into the heart of the country: most notably up into the Clyde at Glasgow, where the tail-end of the great shipbuilding industry is still just twitching. I was sorry to learn that the big oil-rig I saw being completed at Greenock was the yard's last.

The Scottish coast ends undramatically but delightfully on the shores of the Solway Firth, partly exposed, partly soft and warm and sheltered after the harsher north-west. Kirkcudbright is the typical southern seaside town – carefully and graciously laid out, its stone and whitewash well maintained, with a good mixture of assets: a castle, an artists' colony, fine houses, and a pretty tree-shaded quay.

Guinard Island

Shieldaig

Portree, Skye

Ullapool, Gruinard, Shieldaig, Portree

Wars and the fear of them have left curious traces up and down the west coast of Scotland. Set in a pretty bay between Little Loch Broom and Loch Ewe is the low, rounded island of Gruinard. This must be the only place in the country where there are no sheep: germ warfare scientists introduced anthrax there during the war and killed them all. It is still unsafe for sheep and people. On the other hand, the attractive village of Shieldaig owes its very existence to the Napoleonic wars, when it was specially built from scratch to ensure for the Navy a supply of skilful west-coast sailors. Nowadays it is a quiet and unruffled place. Portree has plenty of pleasure boats; but it was only at Ullapool that the existence of a vigorous fishing industry seemed to me strikingly evident, the bright colours of the boats and the oilskins giving life to the greys and grey-blues of the concrete quay and Loch Broom.

Landing Lobsters, Ullapool

Uig and the ferry for Uist

The Calmac ferry

Lochmaddy

South Uist

North and South Uist

Lochmaddy, the northerly of the two Uist ports, is hidden away among many small islands and the landscape consists of an astonishingly complicated mixture of seawater and peat bog. The landscape reminded me of Donegal – the same dark bog crossed and recrossed by telegraph poles, the same careful and laborious activity of cutting out the turf and stacking it to dry out.

On South Uist some of the cottages still have turf roofs, lashed down against the weather just like the stooks of hay standing in the wet fields. Most of the Uist buildings though are more ordinary: severe but solid-looking bungalows, sometimes with painted tin roofs which look good against the threatening skies. I stayed overnight in one of them, comfortably and inexpensively, and was offered friendly and shrewd conversation in the evening and an excellent breakfast ready for the early boat back.

Benbecula near Creagorry

Loch Maddy, North Uist

Uist colours are those of grass and rust, black peat and the changing colours of the sky. This view, looking north-east from just outside Lochmaddy village, might be across an inland loch but the water is really tidal, an arm of Loch Maddy. The careful work visible in the lines of cut and drying turf has been done by hand, but apart from an occasional passing car I saw no one while I was there. The distant hills are those of Harris, beyond the Sound of Berneray. On a hill nearby are some ancient standing stones; but if they are signposted it is so discreetly done that I could not find them at all. Clearly this was mainly due to my own inefficiency, but it also seemed in keeping with the self-sufficient and withdrawn character of Uist.

Loch Maddy, North Uist

The Fairy Isles of Loch Sween, and Loch Craignish

Further down the west coast of the mainland the most delightful landscapes were those where I was amazed less by stupendousness than by delicacy and by detail. This spread and the two following are of places I saw during a week's sailing off the coast of Argyll – partly for fun, partly to see what the coast looked like from the sea. I first saw Loch Sween, *above*, with a considerable sense of relief after what seemed to me a boisterous hour or two tacking to and fro across the Sound of Jura in a stiff breeze. The loch was sheltered and calm, and at its head, by Knapdale Forest, were a number of pretty promontories and islets called the Fairy Isles. The water was dark but clear; the bare waterside rocks led up into

woodland which was lush with grasses and ferns; fallen trees gave it a sense of being untrodden and untended, a place of mystery.

The islands in Loch Craignish, *below*, are bigger and look more solid than the Fairy Isles since in their more exposed position they have fewer trees. The surrounding hills too have a sculptured look, swirling and spiraling up to prominent summits. The place offers a sheltered anchorage for yachts, and also for the fish farms whose metal tanks can often be seen in similarly protected and not-too-inaccessible waters. The fish tanks stay put permanently, whereas the glitter and gleam of the yachts' metal masts and white hulls disappear out to sea during the day.

Mull and Islay

These three sketches were made from a boat swinging gently at anchor in a landlocked haven on the Ross of Mull. It is a confusing way to draw, for the view has shifted every time you look up. The surrounding rocks and hillsides were wild and almost trackless, and I remember the tranquillity and the loneliness of the place with a certain sense of wonder. Some of the pinkish and fern-clad rocks lay in forms that suggested elasticity, even life: not that they resembled anything living but that here and there their repeating forms looked articulated, almost spinal.

The eastern side of Islay facing Jura is so blank and featureless that the mere presence amid such gloomy isolation of the lighthouse on McArthur's Head is quite reassuring. The summit of the mountain behind it, Glas Bheinn, is sometimes clear, sometimes misted; from the sea its foreshortened peat-covered slopes seem to rise almost vertically from the low grey cliffs at its base. No dwellings can be seen. Further up the sound of Jura I saw its three mountains, the Paps of Jura, with solid cloud flowing over them like cream out of a jug.

Ross of Mull

Ross of Mull

86 Ross of Mull

Lighthouse, McArthur's Head, 1

Eilean Mor

Between Jura and the mainland peninsula
of Knapdale lies a group of small and
uninhabited islands. The outermost and
biggest of these, Eilean Mor, is still small
enough to walk round in an hour or so.
In the middle stands a half-ruined chapel.
A little way away are the remains of the
entrance to a hermit's cell, though only a
few courses of it are left. Trying to visualize
a hermit's existence here was not easy.
For a bit, I loved the loneliness and the
peacefulness of this deserted island and the
sounds of the oyster-catchers and seagulls,
but only because my family were nearby
with their specks of bright oilskin on the
grey and the green, and the children's cries
of interest and pleasure at the strangeness
of the place.

chapel, Eilean Mor

Hermit's cell, Eilean Mor

Cell and cliffs, Eilean Mor

Eilean Mor and Corr Eilean

Port Glasgow and Holy Loch

Here and there on the west coast you see
evidence of industry that has come and gone –
on Loch Kishorn for example lie the
remnants of an oil-rig construction site
which took over the untouched landscape,
occupied and used it for a bit, and then
abandoned it as you might abandon an old
bedstead or a clapped-out van. But of all
the west coast's deep indentations, all its
complicated lochs and inlets and rivers, only
the most southerly – the Clyde – has become
heavily industrialized and then stayed that
way over any length of time. There are still
shipyard derricks to be seen at Glasgow, but
only downstream at Port Glasgow did I see
a metal ship actually being built, the first
since the Wallsend cruiser. Its red undercoat
is seen here half hidden behind the grey
stonework of Newark Castle, drawn from
the end of a fenced-off deserted pier. A bit
further on the rig *Ocean Alliance* stood
proudly in its yard, a striking piece of
engineering, handsome in fresh black-and-
grey paintwork with the pipes exposed
Rogers-fashion.

Newark Castle and Port Glasgow

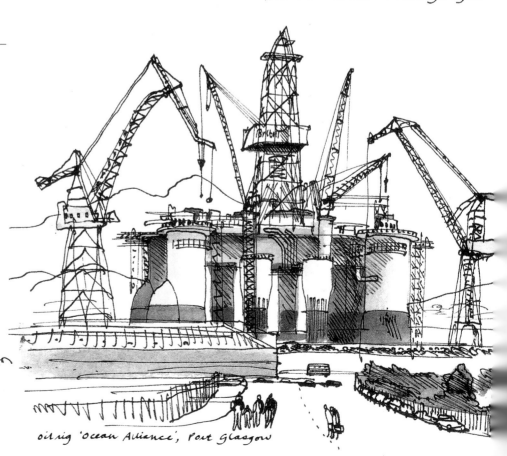

oil-rig 'Ocean Alliance', Port Glasgow

The Holy Loch from Sandbank

As a boy I went down the Clyde once or twice on a paddle-steamer and can remember the spectacle of the moving parts – the pounding silvery pistons inside, the foaming paddle-wheels outside. I also remember keeping some white, slightly translucent lumps of rock of the kind found on the beach at Rothesay or Kilmun. So, out of curiosity, I took the ferry from Gourock to Dunoon. It was another red-funnelled Calmac motor ship. The weather was sunny and there was a pleasant mid-August holiday air all the way to the neat and modestly decorated if rather old fashioned resort of Dunoon.

A mile or two up the coast is Sandbank, from where one can look across the water of Holy Loch to the line of villas opposite on the shore at Kilmun, just visible on the right of the drawing above. My great-uncle owned one of these, 'Lake Villa'. In front of them, though, is a curious sight: the big floating dock and the depot ship for the American nuclear submarine base. Looking for somewhere to stop and draw, I parked by mistake in a surprisingly large and tidy car park with parking bays marked 'Officers only', surrounded by a white fence which four youthful and crew-cut Tom Sawyers in jeans and tee-shirts were painting whiter

still. They were country boys from Oregon and Washington, amicable and cheerful. They pointed out with innocent and proprietorial pride the big black submarine by the floating dock; a couple of them were going off to Glasgow that evening to get tattooed. Even so, all this American metal – supply ship, dry dock, tenders, cranes and derricks, missiles and submarine – struck a jarring note against the Scottish hillsides. I reflected that although the pretext for its being here is the defence of democracy, our consent to this alien presence was no more sought than if we had been Poles or Czechs or East Germans.

Mossyard Bay and Kirkcudbright

The main road from Stranraer to Carlisle is busy, with heavy traffic thundering to
and from the boats for Ireland. But just west of Gatehouse of Fleet where the road passes
through woodland there is a layby and a café, and you can step a few yards down through
the tree trunks on to a wide sandy beach patterned with clumps of marsh grass and a few
rocky outcrops. It is sheltered and warm, the sounds of the road are muffled by the
greenery, and there are fine views across to Sandgreen and out to Fleet Bay and the last big
stretch of open sea before the Solway Firth. A beach like this where trees come down to
the water's edge always has a certain charm. Maybe it reawakens childish memories,
notions of Robinson Crusoe or of stepping ashore on Treasure Island, or maybe it just
reminds me of ads for rum and the West Indies.

Kirkcudbright is pretty and quiet, well laid out with some fine streets, in one of which
the Hornel Art Gallery occupies a handsome and substantial house. It is not surprising
that the town became an artists' and craftsmen's colony; it looks like a good place to put
down roots and keep a respectable tradition going. There is a ruined castle and plenty of
grass to walk on; a few cannon sit around in the shade overlooking the quayside, and the
fishing boats stop the waterside looking too touristy. To the east, at the mouth of the
River Nith, lie Dumfries and Caerlaverock Castle, a remarkable triangular moated castle
of red sandstone, and beyond it the marshes of the Solway Firth and the English border.

MOSSYARD BAY

Kircudbright

Kircudbright

North-West England

The coast of Cumbria is tucked away beyond the Lake District and is rather eclipsed by it. The shore is often very fine. At weekends everyone drives on to the grass by the edge of the sea and peers out at it from behind the wheel. But the towns have seen better days. Maryport, a pretty but sad remnant of a once-considerable port, is becoming a museum, complete with a collection of period shipping. Whitehaven is a run-down but still active industrial harbour, a bit dirty, but with handsome eighteenth-century quays and quayside buildings all in the same brown stone. South of this things get more prosperous but very nuclear. The wildest and bleakest stretch of the entire coast, where the Cumbrian hills slope down to a wide bare shore, is dominated by Sellafield's cooling towers and chimneys; the beach is crossed by ugly and sinister waste outlets which were quite casually allowed to poison the Irish Sea till someone blew the whistle. Barrow-in-Furness was the first shipbuilding town I'd seen which seemed to be really booming, and Barrow's prosperity too is nuclear. Its monster new sheds, put up to build fleets of nuclear submarines, rise above the trim workers' housing of Vickerstown, a kind of industrial Welwyn Garden City waxing fat off our current belligerent frame of mind.

To the east of Barrow, the shores of Morecambe Bay are peaceful again and spectacularly beautiful – partly wooded, partly stone-walled cornfields, stretching down at high tide towards the sea or at low tide towards a vast and lonely landscape of sand. The few towns are old-fashioned. Grange-over-Sands is an agreeably sleepy resort, cut off by the railway from the endless and rather dirty-looking sands beyond. Morecambe has a curious concrete esplanade, stepped like an Indian ghat, and the standard Edwardian amenities – pier, red-brick Winter Garden, clock tower – with the buildings outlined by light bulbs, and the sky festooned with light cables for the Illuminations. Morecambe can never have been particularly smart: now it has a nice, rather shabby feel. But there is nothing run-down about Blackpool, a booming industrial town whose industry is visitors, yet whose warmth and welcome seem friendly. The friendliness may simply be sheer professionalism but it certainly makes you feel at home in your tiny sub-divided bedroom, its half window looking out at close range on to an as yet unilluminated Father Christmas.

To the south of Blackpool lie genteel and grassy Lytham and Southport whose fine beach doubles, economically yet rather squalidly, as a car park and an airstrip. After that, only the pretty Formby sand-dunes separate you from the vast, fascinating and unmanageable sprawl of Liverpool. Here you can see the distinguished relics of a prosperous commercial seaport whose business has lately vanished into thin air, leaving the hardware pointless and reproachful. A small but booming fragment of this prosperity has clung on in the newish Seaforth container dock; upstream a beautiful but now useless collection of nineteenth-century warehouses is being transformed into a vast and extravagant tourist trap complete with a second Tate Gallery. But behind it all lies a run-down and seething hinterland of shabby and burnt-out homes whose occupants have, in the course of all this, been left without anything much to do. Over the city brood the two cathedrals (one decent-looking and substantial, one meretricious), the concrete Beacon Tower, and the two Liver Birds on top of the Liver building. The most delightful thing to do in Liverpool is to take one of the ferries from Pier Head across to Birkenhead and to look back over the water at the fine left-over façades of the once-great port. Its waterfront, like Britain itself, looks fine as long as you keep well back and don't inspect it too closely.

Blackpool: the North Pier and the Tower

Maryport and Whitehaven

Maryport is pretty but sad. Nice white houses stand about on a deserted eighteenth-century quayside. Splendid lock gates swing loose on their hinges at the entrance to the monster Seahouse dock, completely empty; cast-iron bollards stand up in a sea of flowering grass, weeds forcing the stonework apart; even the barbed wire is rusting away. In the inner Elizabeth Dock there are some interesting and curious ships – tugs, an elegant steam launch, a dredger – but their terminal state as maritime museum exhibits only emphasizes the decline of a once-important seaport.

Twelve miles further on, Whitehaven is a curious blend of elegance and squalor. It used to be an important coal, iron and tobacco port and a holiday town. Fine eighteenth-century buildings stand on and around its quaysides, one of which is especially well constructed, with an angled stone ramp shoring up its seaward side and a gracious tower standing at the end like a salt-cellar. Coal tubs and an old tramway locomotive have been placed nearby to stress the town's industrial history, but this is in any case visible on every hand: warehouses, pithead gear, soaring conveyor belts. Whitehaven is not as harmless as it looks: a detergent factory discharges 51 million gallons of chemical waste annually into the Irish Sea, including toxic cadmium and uranium. In 1987 six Greenpeace divers tried to block the pipe but this flow of waste was too strong for them. I had a glass of beer and some chips but avoided the fish.

Maryport

Maryport

Whitehaven

Sellafield and the beach near Drigg

South of St Bees Head the Cumbrian coastal lanes run between deep banks of brambles – not many trees, a few bungalows and caravans, the sea to the right. Ahead, surrounded by deserted and boarded-up farm buildings, are the concrete towers and chimneys of Sellafield: mainly grey, with a few big walls painted red, perhaps for cheerfulness. The view of it from the fields near Seascale to the south is cut off near ground level by 'landscaped' banks of earth giving the foreground the air of an ancient hill fort. The scale is impossible to judge until one uses the minuscule cranes and derricks as a guide. At Drigg, a mile or two further south, the road to the beach skirts a heavily fenced-off, ditched and planted site where low-level radioactive waste is kept until someone can think what to do with it. The beach, which is wide and generally sandy with views of dunes backed by distant moorland fells, is wild and featureless – except that it is crossed by a long waste pipe, heavily strengthened but still battered and uneven in places, which runs from the general direction of the waste site down to the low-water mark.

A little further to the south the shoreline is interrupted by the mouth of the River Esk. Ravenglass on a Sunday morning was very quiet and I thought the beach looked pretty dismal; but for a few manhole covers and a boat it was bare. No weed was growing on the hard pebbly stretches exposed at low tide and there were no sea birds anywhere on this sterile shore.

Sellafield from the beach near Drigg

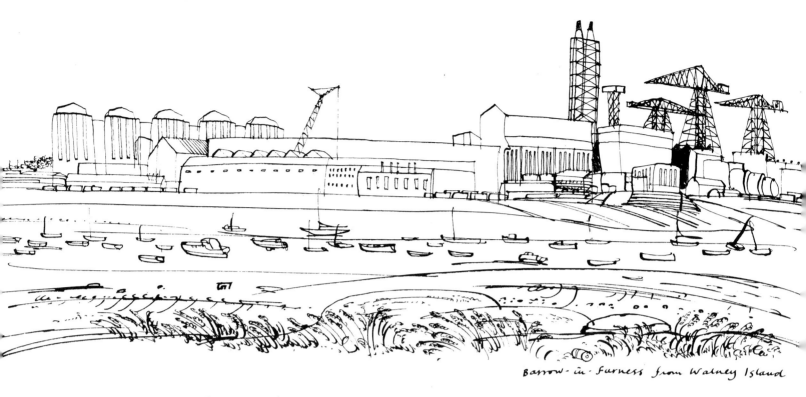

Barrow-in-Furness from Walney Island

Barrow-in-Furness and Morecambe Bay

Walney Channel separates Barrow-in-Furness from the long narrow Isle of Walney which protects it. Ahead is the prosperous-looking Vickers shipyard; in the new sheds on the left Britain's Trident missile submarines are being built. Nothing here looks remotely ramshackle or run-down or starved of funding. This was the only really assured and confident-looking shipyard I saw anywhere round the coast.

At Baycliff near Barrow the harvest fields stretch down between Lakeland drystone walls towards the misty, enigmatic expanses of Morecambe Bay. From here, looking across the sands of Morecambe Bay you can see the big concrete cube of Heysham's nuclear power-station. A mile away from it is a small headland with a Saxon chapel and some curious and rather pathetic graves carved out of the solid rock and filled with rain-water.

Stone graves, Old Heysham

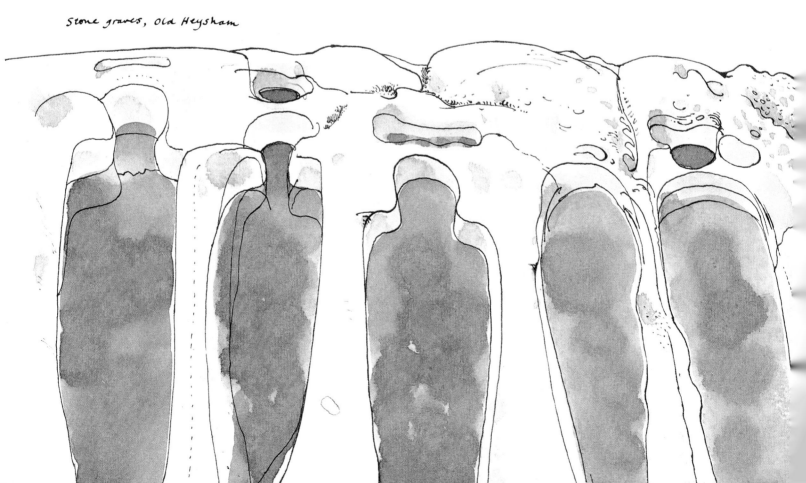

IOI

Baycliff

Morecambe

Morecambe and Southport

At the seaside, all the pressures are now towards brashness; there is no mileage in being refined. At Morecambe, this leads to curious changes of key: between the Winter Gardens' original dignity, for example, and the cheerfully vulgar tat now stuck all over them. Yet you could hardly have described the original red-brick building as restrained. The Winter Gardens look out towards the curving esplanade and the bay through festoons of as yet unlit illuminations. These extend past the shoe-permarket to the clock tower and the pier. I have seen classier pier approaches without necessarily liking them any better: nobody could call this one pretentious or overbearing. This gives it the same charm as Morecambe itself: as timeless, long-suffering and shabby as the strings of donkeys on the beach.

Southport is newer and generally grander and its pier Funland is evidently costing a lot more, though Queen Victoria remains unamused. At her back there is a promenade with grand hotels and smart new flats; with ample Victorian and Edwardian buildings and cast-iron verandahs. In short, away from the shore Southport is socially and architecturally a cut above Morecambe. But it's a pity about the beach. Cars in ads used often to be seen driving across empty and virginal beaches, but never more than one at a time, never taking the place over, parked door-to-door on the sands, as they are here. Southport's long sandy beach is not only a car park but also a landing strip for pleasure flights and a sales area, the vans marked variously Catering Express, Seafood, Beach Shop, Ices Made Specially for You, and Beach Recovery.

Morecambe pier

Morecambe

CHRIST
DIED
FOR
ME
SINS

Welcome to
FUNLAND
CAFE   BAR
BINGO   POOL

Southport

ICE CREAM

The beach at Southport

Blackpool

I had expected Blackpool to be crowded, brash, vulgar, ugly and
rackety; and so it was. But I hadn't expected it also to be friendly,
stylish, interesting, lively, old-fashioned and curiously touching.

Having woken early, I drew the Tower and had a walk along
the Golden Mile and back along the beach before many people
were about. The tide was out, and where it was wet the empty
beach reflected the Tower. Under the North Pier, a man was
preparing a group of seven donkeys for the day's work. Later
in the morning when I did the other drawings, the seats on the
Central Pier were filling up with people enjoying the sun and
reading the papers or doing books full of crosswords. By now
the beach was crammed full, with ice-cream caravans and Land
Rovers as well as people; and as the tide came in, everybody was
forced to retreat up the steps on to the tiered concrete steps of the
promenade, which by midday had taken on the densely packed
appearance of the ghats at Benares. Some people were
determinedly sunbathing, others simply falling asleep in the sun;
and between the pretty Turkish gazebos of the North Pier (the
oldest of the three) people lay fast asleep in the curiously ordered
abandon only possible in neatly ranged lines of deckchairs.
Beyond the pier theatre at the far end, a narrower and lower deck
was almost as crowded, but with anglers. I reflected that, over the
years, Blackpool had certainly made a great many people
extremely happy. There were plenty of other attractions of course:
Lewis's and Pricebusters and Mr B's Amusements; tramrides and
trips in horse-drawn carriages; electronic battles with fearsome
Space Harriers and Sea Harriers; junk food along the Golden Mile
and cheap, friendly fish-and-chip shops only a street or two back
from it. What does it matter if most of the buildings along the
Mile look shoddy or vulgar? No one looks and no one cares.

Blackpool: the central Pier

Blackpool: the Central Pier

Liverpool

I first realized how romantic
the Liverpool docks look while
wandering around them with
my brother more than twenty
years ago. There were still big
ships in the basins, though
everything was at a standstill
because of a long-drawn-out
dockers' or seamen's strike.
Now there are no more strikes;
and, except in the Seaforth
Container Terminal, precious
few dockers or seamen or ships
either. But much of the fine
warehouse architecture
survives, some of it neglected,
some acknowledged as still
usable, some recognized for its
tourist potential.

The best of the dockland
architecture can be seen along
the road that runs from Pier
Head downstream to Bootle.
Some of the warehouses are
masterpieces, monumental in
scale but unemphatic in style,
without bombast. Here and
there you can see what has
replaced the old dockland
activities: container ships that
unload themselves, surrounded
by stacked and self-sufficient
containers. And behind it all, in
Toxteth, you see the desolation
left behind now that Liverpool's
original purpose has shrunk and
shrivelled away.

Dock entrance, Waterloo Road

Bootle

Gateway to Albert Dock

Burnt-out shops in Toxteth

107

Liverpool and the Mersey

The only place to see Liverpool as a whole is from the recently done-up ferry terminal across the Mersey at Birkenhead. From here the long low warehouses look as anonymous as they were meant to; the buildings that cry out for attention are the ones that grab the skyline. The three most striking from anywhere on the river are those at Pier Head: the Royal Liver Insurance Company building whose twin towers are topped by the rather menacing Liver Birds, the lower square Cunard Building, and the domed Dock Board offices. Behind the Albert Dock rises the curious cut-off cone of the Roman Catholic cathedral, a showy architectural lightweight, and to the right the solid and traditional tower of the big Anglican cathedral. The two-way ferryboat trip is a delightful experience, with interesting views of the ex-shipbuilding Birkenhead side of the Mersey as well. But although the Cammell Laird yards are still a prominent feature of the Birkenhead waterfront I couldn't actually see any ships on the stocks.

Conwy Ca

The Coast of Wales

Wales has the strangest, most distinctive, most Celtic and most clearly defined coastline of them all. Many of its smaller coastal buildings are so characteristic of the principality that they seem almost to speak Welsh. Its wildest coastal scenery has a jagged ferocity and a savage desolation unparalleled in Britain.

Its two extremities – the peninsular tips of Gwynedd in the north and Dyfed in the south – are remarkably wild and unspoilt. Its inlets and estuaries are tranquil and beautiful, even where – as at Milford Haven – they accommodate a big industrial element. Indeed, it is the presence of industry, active or residual, that gives a special character and interest to many Welsh ports and harbours: Porthgain is a typical instance. A fine collection of ancient Edwardian castles stands on Wales's shores commanding the most strategic positions, even if – as at Rhuddlan and Kidwelly – the sea has since retreated from them. And a splendid array of seaside towns and villages has grown up, often as the result of inspired and far-sighted entrepreneurs, to provide for the visitor's needs.

But Wales begins and ends badly. From Prestatyn through Rhyl and Abergele to Colwyn Bay and Rhos-on-Sea extends the undistinguished and jazzed-up waterfront of a string of holiday towns without much previous architectural character, unbroken except where they peter out into a no-man's-land of holiday barracks, chalets and recent ribbon-development bungalows, all of them as tacky and impermanent-looking as the monster window-to-window caravan sites that fill in the gaps between them. It all has the regimented and thrusting yet seedy appearance of developments that have enriched the few at the expense of the many. The best way to see it is from the merciful motorway which whisks you obliviously past it all to the beauties of Llandudno.

Llandudno in the north and Tenby in the south-west are two of my favourite seaside towns: Llandudno for the majestic way its fine gleaming stucco terraces follow the curving sweep of the shore round to the pier and the beginning of Great Orme Head, all façade and none the worse for it; Tenby for the altogether more informal way in which its steeper streets and smaller terraces curl around their twin-fronted promontory. Llandudno looks like a more sinuous Brighton, but architecturally Tenby reflects characteristic Welsh virtues: in its use both of dark stonework and painted stucco, and in its innate elegance, often using classical motifs but in an inventive and exuberant way, so that the façades of quite ordinary houses often have an emphatic individuality as well as a robust Welsh bravura.

The western part of Gwynedd is the emptiest bit of the coast, and the extreme tip of the Lleyn peninsula beyond Aberdaron is the finest scenically. Looking over the Lleyn from a vantage point on one of its curved hills, it appears an idyllic landscape, its gently rounded modelling emphasized as the land slips away by the pattern of small walled fields and white farm buildings spreading smoothly away to a blue sea dotted with flat islets. Its beaches are long, empty sweeps of sand and it all looks as the loveliest parts of Cornwall must have looked about sixty years ago. It seemed, on the day I saw it, a peaceful reminder; whereas in the south, the rocky tips of Dyfed around St David's and beyond Milford Haven are rugged in the extreme, with the fiercest and most spectacular cliff scenery I've seen anywhere.

This Pembroke coast is altogether wilder, harsher, than the north, its cliffs a jagged wilderness of rock and foam, its skylines more broken and pointed, its islands bleaker and more isolated. But penetrating this cruel coastline are crevices and inlets and havens of charm or great beauty, enhanced by all the delightful and appropriate paraphernalia of boats and quaysides, lime-kilns and cliff paths, groups and terraces of whitewashed Welsh cottages.

The prettiest features of the Welsh coast are the harbours, especially those at Fishguard, Aberaeron and Tenby where the sands shrink or swell with the tide below a curving background of rock, stonework and painted plaster. The most agreeable things people have added to the landscape are the older, sparkling buildings, in dark stone; and the remote towns whose chemists' are called Medical Halls and whose railways still run by steam across long wooden bridges or up steep woodland valleys of rock and fern.

The good and bad things about the coast of South Wales are to do with coal: as a fuel for the steelworks and the industrial landscapes of the coastal strip near Port Talbot, and as a pretext – now vanished – for the specially built anthracite port of Cardiff. Port Talbot is magnificent at dusk or at night; when you can see only its floodlights and its burning flares, it looks like a romantic nineteenth-century vision of the Spirit of Industry. But by day, if you can be bothered to penetrate the industrial estates of Aberavon to the beach, it is remarkable only for its extreme dreariness: a razed concrete landscape, a sort of low concrete pier you're not supposed to go on, and beaches of dirty and coal-blackened sand. The remains of Cardiff's docks are stranger and more haunting, because of their fine architectural remnants – two warehouses standing by the big new field where the filled-in dock used to be, and a splendid Pilotage building still standing amid the dockland semaphores by the old harbour entrance. The rich mixture of old and new, viable and done-for, natural and artificial, is essentially Welsh. There are many instances of it, often where you least expect them, all round this curious and unpredictable coast.

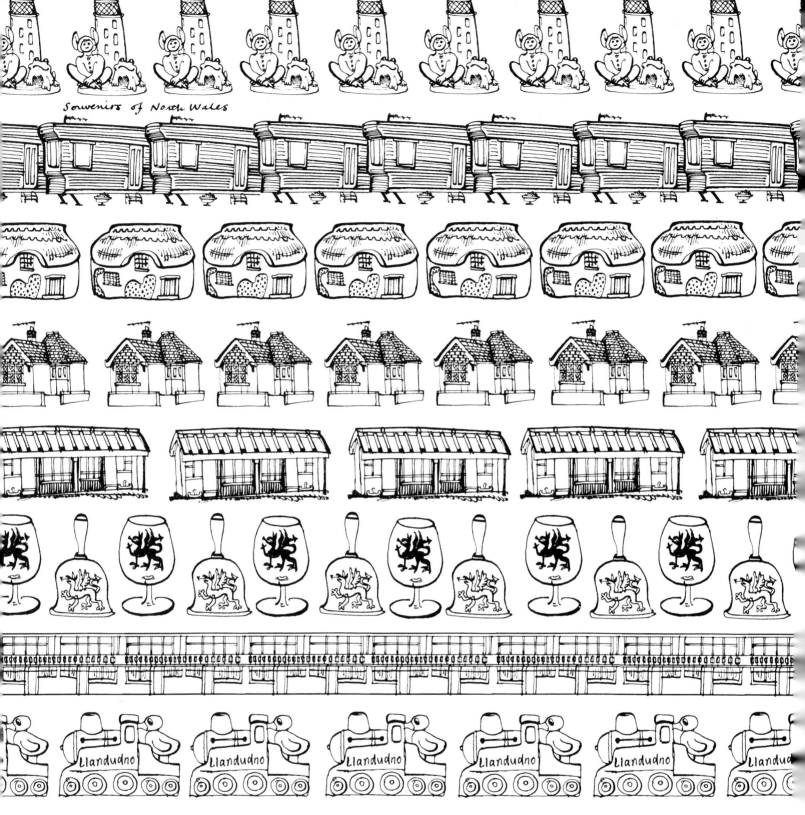

Souvenirs of North Wales

Prestatyn to Llandudno

These caravans, bungalows and terraced holiday homes may be seen along the roads between Prestatyn and Colwyn Bay; the other things may be bought from a kiosk on Llandudno pier. This pier still looks in good shape, the delicate iron structure, cast-iron railings and elegant pavilions all well cared for. Llandudno's long curving terraces too look prosperous and distinguished. They were built as a speculative venture by Edward Mostyn and Owen Williams, about 1850 – at about the time when Belgravia was being completed – and they have something of the same splendour.

Beyond the pier rises the great limestone lump of the Great Orme, the headland which really marks the end of the north coast of Wales. It has the same skeletal and exposed rockiness as parts of the Pennines, and the same sparkle when the limestone catches the sun. From the top the coast is visible stretching away towards the Dee and the Mersey. Industrial Lancashire is no further away from here than London is from Clacton or Margate, so it's not surprising that the intervening coastline looks so thoroughly used-up.

Llandudno: Orme Head

Llandudno

Beaumaris

Beaumaris

The Menai Straits

Moelfre

Wylfa

Puffin Island

Anglesey

Anglesey owes its most spectacular aspects to Ireland: without the Irish connection there would be no A5, no Telford, no Menai Straits Bridge, no Holyhead and no South Stack. This lighthouse sits at Anglesey's western extremity. It is, like many of them, as interesting for the pattern its walls make on the rough terrain as for the lighthouse itself. From the cliffs nearby you can look down on South Stack and watch the Irish boat disappearing in the haze and the small fishing boats plodding back into port; and then you can turn and survey the deserted landscapes of Holy Island and the south-west coast of Anglesey, an undramatic grey-green countryside sloping down to the Irish Sea.

But on Anglesey there are plenty of other delightful if less astonishing things to see: the Beaumaris waterfront for instance, with its pretty verandahs and tame herring gulls strutting and screaming, and its outlook across the sandy Menai Straits towards the slopes of Snowdonia; and the waterside at Moelfre, agreeably

composed of black rock, grey shingle, white houses and coloured boats, nothing special but pleasantly ordinary and undamaged. I noted the odd contrasts around the nuclear power-station at Wylfa: the roofless ruins of a big abandoned farmhouse on the Cemaes side; on the western, the rocky outcrops, drystone walls and gentle green slopes, with in each case the monster plant puffing and steaming away against the background of the sea – a feature whose safety one just has to take on trust. Such a scene has become a standard feature of the coastline. By contrast, the most noticeable aspect of a landscape may merely be its emptiness and loneliness, as at Black Point near Penmon, Anglesey's eastern tip. There may be a car or two parked in the grass and a group of orange-jacketed canoeists paddling back from Puffin Island past the striped, chess-queen lighthouse to the café. But the hollow tolling clang of the bell buoy makes Penmon seem a withdrawn and mysterious place where we are all only temporary intruders.

The Lleyn Peninsula

Parts of the Lleyn peninsula are the wildest and least exploited bits of the Welsh coastline. If you arrive out of season at Trevor, a small beach on the north coast, you feel like the only visitor it has ever had. The tractor makes the beach look agricultural, more like a bit of farmland than anything connected with holidaymaking. And if you climb the rocky high ground at Mynydd Mawr on its western tip and look down on the surrounding moorland, fields, lanes and farmhouses, you see a landscape of timeless serenity descending gently to the sea. At the very top is a coastguard hut: you can peep in and see the two essentials, binoculars and kettles.

In the crook of this headland is Aberdaron, a pleasant whitewashed village with the usual amenities of pub, hotel, café, a little stream and a red-and-white-painted naval mine. The long beach is overlooked by a churchyard full of purply-grey slate. The flat graves have lengthy and beautifully lettered inscriptions in both English and Welsh, but no pictures or decorative flourishes – tempting me to conclude that the Welsh are only really interested in words. Abersoch is a much more booming and present-day sort of place, full of power-boating with its bric-à-brac of parked trailers and expensively modernized holiday homes. Pwllheli and Criccieth are older places, still served by a railway. Criccieth has a fine castle and a nice pebbly beach where around breakfast time ladies walk their dogs.

Criccieth

Trevor and Gwm Ddu

Abersoch

Aberdaron churchyard

The Lleyn Peninsula from Mynydd Mawr

A berystwyth

Aberaeron

Aberystwyth and Newquay

Like Llandudno's, the front at Aberystwyth curves gently round a shallow bay. Between a cliff railway and a pier which has seen better days runs a pleasant strip of ice-cream-coloured three- and four-storey houses and hotels, broken in the middle by an emphatic vertical feature, the clock tower of the Neuadd y Brenin or King's Hall. The tower is painted in strawberry and vanilla, and the clock faces lack hands. Beyond the pier is the university, a fine and individual Gothic-revival building, standing just back from a magnificent esplanade, one of the handsomest survivors in this noteworthy seaside tradition.

Aberaeron and Newquay are opposites, though both are delightful nineteenth-century creations. Aberaeron, the earlier of the two, has the controlled but expansive beauty of a place built especially to look elegant: the Regency houses are ranged round the big square harbour and up the river. At Newquay, the quay itself is what gave the village its being, with its curves, ramps and various levels. But the terraces that spread behind it have a more utilitarian look to them: those on the right look like the orderly terraces one sees in the mining valleys, machines for other people to live in. Newquay is supposed to have been the original model for *Under Milk Wood*, but it is more discreet about the relationship than Laugharne, which rather cashes in on it.

Newquay   121

Ceibwr Bay and Porthgain

Beyond Cardigan the coast is wild and magnificent. The sea is a backdrop to rolling farmland, whose trees and bushes are stunted and shaped to the fierce winds, and the lanes are sunk deep into the fields, as if sheltering: a few farmhouses here and there give a sense of scale. West of Cardigan the landscape changes to a bleaker, browner key, in which the few villages provide pleasant accents of black and white. At Porthgain this curious and picturesque landscape has been left behind after the death fifty or sixty years ago of the local industry of granite quarrying and crushing. The ruined plant is not particularly ancient: the brick and concrete of the big crusher are clearly twentieth-century, and although the fine jetty is much older, parts of it have been strengthened and rebuilt in efficient if inhuman concrete. You might think there had hardly been time for Porthgain to become picturesque at all – everything here is still hard-edged and raw. But the used-up relics of industry are just as much a thing of the past as the nineteenth-century lime-kilns on the Welsh quaysides and the ruined Edwardian castles. The rocky coast on either side reminds me of north Cornwall, but is barer of houses. No wonder the place is glad of its visitors: it would be badly off without them.

Porth-clais

St David's and Marloes

Western Dyfed has two prongs, both rocky and inhospitable. But the more northerly, centring on St David's, is penetrated by two pretty inlets where boats can shelter: the tiny Porth-clais and the bigger Solva which is a substantial but secluded natural harbour. There are grassy jetties on both sides of the River Solva; that on the east has a row of old lime-kilns. A beautiful path, half-hidden under hedges, climbs the hill to the left of the drawing until you can see down into another small bay and out to the open sea.

The more southerly prong is near Marloes, west of Milford Haven. There is a fine sandy beach, broken with fierce rocks, but the most spectacular views are of rock and water alone: a wilderness of cruel rock forms with only the distant outline of Skomer Island to relieve it. These three landscapes have been secured by the imagination and forethought of the National Trust, which early realized that unless action was taken the Dyfed coast would soon face the same threats as Devon and Cornwall.

Solva

Rocks at Marl

pembroke Castle

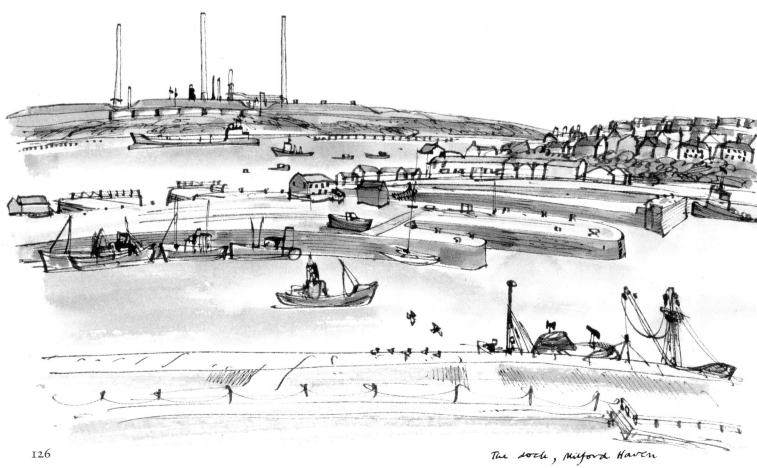

The dock, Milford Haven

Milford Haven and the Gower Peninsula

Just beyond Marloes is the entrance to the finest and most
extensive inlet of them all – Milford Haven. Until about twenty-
five years ago it was extremely beautiful: nine miles of open deep
water leading up to the old whaling port of Milford Haven and
beyond it to a further network of tidal inlets of unique length and
complexity. The Haven was flanked by the gentle slopes of an
unbroken rural landscape and was penetrated by tranquil creeks
and landlocked bays. Nothing impinged on this landscape.
Refineries arrived in the early sixties, amid much public outcry;
their steel chimneys are inescapable, sticking up at you like
periscopes over the sands and beyond the old grassy dock
quaysides. These tall chimneys and the silvered cylinders of the
oil storage drums are what the landscape now *is*. Wondering if
they look nice or not is pretty pointless.

Milford Haven from Dale

Pennard cliffs, Gower peninsula

Parts of the Gower Peninsula's beautiful southern coastline live
with a similar if more insidious threat: the stealthy creeping up
of suburbia as near as it dares to the cliff edge. But if you clamber
a few feet down the sloping cliffs you completely forget it and
imagine that Gower consists only of majestic stone and turf,
gently breaking waves and croaking ravens.

Tenby

Tenby is quite simply the best-looking and most agreeable seaside town in Britain. Its streets and lanes are a pleasure to walk about in; its pretty buildings and its quaysides snake around a fine sandy harbour; it has two waterfronts, each quite different in character, and several beaches; the mixture of old seaport and watering place and present-day prosperity is easy and unstrained; many of its individual buildings are fascinating architecturally; it is neither spoilt nor decayed; there are many good things to look at in the town, and Caldey Island offers a pretext for a delightful boat trip.

The island is rocky and lonely. The only creatures to be seen here are seals and monks, but my children and I glimpsed neither.

The Pembrokeshire coast just to the west of Tenby is very fine, with a beautiful gorse-covered headland at Lydstep Point and the Norman castle of Manorbier just beyond it. At its southernmost point there are dramatic cliffs and the spray-pounded Elegug rock stacks. Down in a crevice in the rock, almost at water level, is the small and touching chapel of St Govan. But west from here, the coast has been given over to the military for tank-training.

The harbour at Tenby

Caldey Island

130 Port Talbot

Caldey Island, Laugharne and Aberavon

Caldey Island's columnar rock forms and grassy slopes are about as close as one can get to an unspoilt landscape: nothing but seals and seagulls and the occasional putter of a boat. Laugharne's castle, though it must once have seemed new and impressive, looks by now almost as untouched: broken walls and clefts and crevices, all formed and shaped as much by time as by people.

The coastal views near Port Talbot, looking along the flat coastal strip from Aberavon towards Margam Burrows, are much more extraordinary; what has happened here in recent years has changed the shape of everything. Here and there are striking (or perhaps merely new and unfamiliar) structures, things of such

unusual shape and function that they seem grotesque or bizarre. The whole scene can look very pretty, puffing and hissing and gleaming and essential-looking. Or again it can look thoughtlessly destructive and out of control, like a child's playroom when a tidy-up is overdue.

Aberavon itself is a newly created holiday resort of distressing seediness. Before ending up at Aberavon beach I had tried at various places along this stretch of coast to get through the industrial areas to the sea, but was usually thwarted by roads that ended in wired-off and waterlogged no-go zones where willow-wrens sang over a wasteland of scattered plastic and paper rubbish.

Cardiff Docks

Good valley coal made Cardiff, and most of it was exported through the docks built for the purpose by the second Marquis of Bute in early Victorian times. Now these once extensive docks are interesting but forlorn. The long basin which penetrated almost to the centre of the city has been filled in and grassed over, leaving a couple of handsome Victorian warehouses high and dry at the edge of a new monster field. At the old dock entrance stands the handsome Pilotage building facing the mud and the tides of the outer dock. Out on the mud stand several dolphins, heavy free-standing wooden structures which carried the signalling devices for ships entering port. These too look desolate; indeed, disused signals often do look sad and sinister, like incomprehensible gestures and mumblings, or like the enigmatic structures on the skyline in the paintings of the Surrealists and of Bosch and Brueghel.

Walled up in the mouth of the dock lies an old Bristol Channel tugboat, becalmed now amid weeds and bushes. Other disused vehicles and bits of machinery have been collected in the adjoining Industrial and Maritime Museum. There are fine buildings in the now rather run-down streets nearby – banks and offices which have been left behind by comparison with prosperous central Cardiff, but which reflect the high standards and ambitions of the late-nineteenth-century port.

Bristol Channel tug-boat, Cardiff

Cardiff

Cardiff: warehouses and filled-in dock

Pilotage building, Cardiff Docks

The South - West

I've always loved the south-western peninsula of England. As a boy I had several holidays there; in between visits, vivid pictures of it stayed in my mind. And although many of the things I liked best now seem picturesque, overrun and commercialized, for me it remains the first place where I saw rocky cliffs and deep blue water, ferny ravines and open seaside moorland, ravens and Atlantic rollers, fishing boats and whitewashed villages; the place where I tasted clotted cream and sweet cider and crab salad, noticed how many flowers there were in the deep lanes, and saw how the Atlantic winds could shape the trees. It was in South Devon that I first set foot in a small boat; clambered aboard a wrecked windjammer; and, after a fruitless mackerel-fishing expedition with my father, was first seasick. Certain incidents from long ago still remain especially clear. I remember cycling with my brother along the coastal road in West Penwith and picnicking on top of one of the thick field walls within sight of the blue sea. There were cowpats in the roadway but when our precious rationed sandwiches fell near one of them we ate them all the same; for the rest of that holiday I worried that we might have caught polio from it. I remember a walk down beaches and over giant rocks from St Just to Land's End; walking over the clifftops from Lyme Regis to Charmouth and returning along the rock-strewn beach; cycling round the south coast of the Isle of Wight before the days of Amusements in the chines, and catching the ferry across the still water from Yarmouth to Lymington in the calm evening. I spent a pre-war Devon holiday in an ex-gipsy caravan set down by a sandy cove near Salcombe, when the deep banks of the lush midsummer lanes were full of campions and heavy with snails. And there were many outings by bike in the traffic-free roads of 1950 from the Bodmin army camp: to Wadebridge and Padstow, Tintagel and Rock, Looe and Fowey and Mevagissey. One long evening cycle run to Polperro at midsummer is especially vivid in my mind: as the landscape darkened a full moon came out and the Cornish hills and hedgerows looked like a painting by Samuel Palmer.

The south-west is generally thought the most idyllic and most picturesque region of England. This is certainly how I thought of it, brought up on haphazard bits of *Westward Ho!*, Hardy, *Lorna Doone*, Quiller-Couch, Daphne du Maurier, Virginia Woolf and John Betjeman. I also knew of the traditional artists of the Newlyn School and the romantic St Ives painters of my youth – Christopher Wood, Ben Nicolson, Alfred Wallis and Bryan Wynter.

After Brunel's romantic Bristol and the splendid sands of Weston-super-Mare the villages get fewer, smaller and prettier, the cliffs taller and more rugged – Hartland Point

especially so. The north Cornish coast is very fine, the granite only thinly clad with turf and in early summer pink with thrift; the most magical stretch of all is the far tip, West Penwith. The southern Cornish coast and South Devon are milder and softer. Dartmouth is full of retired naval men with spyglasses looking from bay windows. The South Devon soil is warm tinted from red sandstone – you see it from the train in the cliffs at Dawlish. Dorset cliffs are creamy at Golden Cap, grey at Portland, and white near Lulworth and at Studland where the chalk first surfaces.

Cornwall is the most extreme and the most vulnerable part of the peninsula, being the part most threatened by the holiday business. Yet for some years after the war, though magical enough, it was grey and run-down. When I was there in the Army its seaside villages were so unspoilt that you could not get a cup of tea. In pre-war days, the people who knew and cared about Cornwall and had the means and the time regularly to take their holidays there were professional or academic. They took the Cornish Riviera Express and, for their long holidays, built the white-painted and grey-roofed houses that stand in discreet numbers on the turf above the beaches. I had two or three nights in one of these houses, at Treyarnon Bay, after it had become a youth hostel. Later on, when more people had cars, Cornwall began bursting at the seams. The National Trust was the first to see the likely threat to this coastline and began protecting it, concentrating on the south-western peninsula to such good effect that it has preserved 33 per cent of the Cornish coastline, 30 per cent of Devon's. But even so it has proved vulnerable, as the beauty and the romantic appeal of the region has been more and more popularized and exploited. After a point, romance and tourism don't go together.

Here, more than anywhere else in the country, you know that as a visitor your role has changed. Instead of being the inconspicuous observer of the various fascinating activities that used to sustain the place and give it interest, the visitor has now become merely the raw material in the only really profitable industrial process left, tourism: an essential raw material maybe, but an unloved one, which has to be firmly held at bay by double yellow lines, faraway car parks and blank looks, to be serviced as efficiently and speedily as possible with pasties, cream teas and fudge and ensnared in 'antique' shops as cunningly baited and unavoidable as the lobster pots ranged on the quay. Meanwhile, as the herring gulls riffle through the car-park litter bins, the fine deep-water inlets fill with laid-up oil tankers and retired drilling-rigs, the clifftops with caravans, and the access motorways with stationary traffic.

...st Pool from Messack

Bristol

Although all but one of the old ships have gone, Bristol's quaysides still remain and you can with a little effort imagine how the port might once have looked: masts and sails, rigging and funnels crowded together only just across a narrow jetty from the warehouses and the dockside streets of this remarkable city. You can walk down the steep hill from the suspension bridge and along the river, past several enormous tobacco warehouses glowing pink in the haze, and past the old dock entrance off the main river. It is hard to believe that this muddy-banked waterway could ever have coped with such a vast flow of trade.

The least-changed feature of the city is the suspension bridge over the Avon Gorge at Clifton. With an autumn haze to prevent one seeing too much of the distant detail, this scene still looks much as it must always have looked. Its designer Brunel never saw the bridge completed, but he had already played a crucial role in Bristol's history, having been personally responsible for building the railway, the main station and the docks. He also designed and built the steamship *Great Britain*, built originally for the Bristol transatlantic run, and now back in her original dock, well restored externally after eighty years as a forgotten hulk in the Falklands. Although I'm in principle a bit cool about the sanctifiction of our Heritage, since it often distracts us from adjusting to the realities of the present, it is an interesting experience to descend the steps deep down into the old dry dock, its fine stone walls as firmly laid as a castle's, and look up at the bulging lines of Brunel's sturdy iron hull, here where it was built.

Weston-super-Mare

I had never seen Weston-super-Mare before, but it looked familiar. On a grey late-August day it had all the empty expanse of sand and all the chilliness you can't help associating with the British seaside. Trapnell Sons Donkey Rides 30p were doing slow business; children in groups or in pairs cycled along on canopied four-wheelers; a few families were playing on the pretty tree-shaded putting-green in front of the Richmond Hotel, or bouncing on one of the familiar inflatable castles; elderly people sheltered in the stone bays along the esplanade or on the pier benches, close together as if for warmth and reassurance; the driver of the pier tractor-train was debating with the pier manager whether it was getting too wet to run one more trip before lunch; space invaders, dodgems, ghost train and bingo were going full tilt in the big amusements shed at the far end of the pier.

The North Devon Coast

Ilfracombe's hotels make a visitor feel like a lobster choosing a lobster pot: each so tempting and so like the next; why not just pop in and have a quick look?

The first North Devon town I ever saw was Lynmouth, just after walking down the enchanting woodland gorge of the Lyn from Watersmeet. This was before the disastrous flood, and the best things about Lynmouth now are still the pre-flood relics. The cliff railway, running up and down through its tunnel of ferns, must be the prettiest anywhere; the lime-kilns on the quayside are, as they always seem to be, solid and satisfying to look at; the old hotels climbing up into the woods are durable and handsome. But the thatched ice-cream stall and the new tower on the jetty lack the magic touch.

Ilfracombe and Clovelly are both built round or above harbours – Ilfracombe a seaside town on the grand scale, Clovelly a tiny and strictly preserved village. Each is in its own way unique: Ilfracombe for its style and its unquestioning self-confidence, Clovelly for the natural and unforced way its picturesqueness has arisen simply from its being stuck on a very steep hill, kept free of traffic and painted white. At its lower end is a most beautiful structure: a perfectly maintained stone harbour which is a delight to walk on. There is another fine lime-kiln at Buck's Mills near Clovelly, looking like an overgrown Mediterranean fortress stuck half-way up a cliff edge and almost like an extension of the cliff itself. The coast hereabouts is splendid: extensive sand dunes at Braunton Burrows; well-clad and rocky cliffs at Combe Martin, like one of Gainsborough's imaginary romantic landscapes made out of sticks and stones and bits of material; bare and mean-looking cliffs at Hartland Point. These last prepare one for the even more desolate coast of North Cornwall.

Ilfracombe harbour

Lynmouth: lime kiln

Lynmouth

Lynmouth: cliff railway

Lynmouth

Clovelly

Lynmouth

Lynmouth

Clovelly

Ilfracombe

Buck's Mills

Combe Martin

Hartland Point

141

Morwenstow

Morwenstow, Tintagel and Bedruthan Steps

Cornwall begins with a landscape of vividly contrasting elements: the gently patterned and rolling hillsides near Morwenstow, crossed by an old green lane shaded by low and windswept oaks, and beyond it the attentive dishes of the listening station near Lower Sharpness Point which G C H Q shares with its American counterpart N S A. On a headland eighteen miles south is another landmark equally steeped in legend and mystery, though of an older sort: the ruined castle of Tintagel, whose outermost island crag is entered through this archway. Beyond it are unforgettable views of weather-lashed rocks and terrifying spray-filled abysses. Like the first two scenes, the third also contains an intrusive element. But the monster rocks at Bedruthan Steps, though equally striking, are entirely natural: huge stacks of hard granite left standing on a golden beach, facing a fierce and relentless sea. This strangely contrasting scene of rock castles built on sand yet standing firm is one of Cornwall's most memorable.

Tintagel

Bedruthan Steps

143

West Penwith

West Penwith's most remarkable feature
is the balance between the forbidding
landscape and the works of farmers and
miners – a balance which suggests a
partnership in which neither is over-
whelmed. Its most enduring signs are the
intricate patterns of the field walls, deep
structures of stone and earth which overlay
the green countryside. But its distinctive
features are the relics, now wholly disused,
of the copper and tin mining industry: the
pithead winding gear and the engine houses
which powered the pumps needed to stop
the mines flooding. The cliff-edge engine
at Botallack served a mine stretching deep
under the sea; beyond it the coast becomes
purely rural, its landmarks the great
outcrops of granite rock in which man's
hand has played no part at all.

Engine House, Botallack

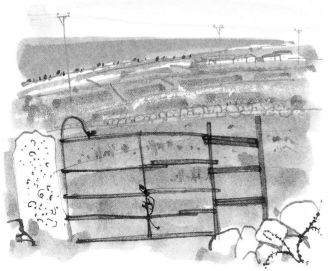

Near Zennor

Morvah

Geevor Mine

Near Rosemergy

Cape Cornwall

Treryn Dinas

Kynance Cove, the Lizard

Cadgwith and Mevagissey

The scene on the left is what draws visitors to Cornwall, but the one above is what they probably find. Cadgwith is only a few miles away from the fierce and terrible Lizard (pp. 146–7). It has all the characteristics of the traditional fishing cove of the imagination: a tranquil place, protected by a headland from the sea's full fury, with its attention still firmly centred on its original business of catching fish. A pretty path, lushly overgrown in summer, winds from the car park past a chapel made of grey corrugated iron, and by some thatched cottages, on to a shingle beach surrounded by stone buildings. The pinpoints of colour come from red ridge tiles, yellow lichens and the blues and reds of the boats on the beach. In its early June greenery before the summer season is properly begun it looks delightful.

The quayside at Mevagissey has vitality of a different order. As a student I came here from time to time and thought it perfect. One of my first commissions was to draw a lithograph of this scene as it then was: a fishing boat at the quay, some fishermen, the same houses rising up the far hillside. Late one evening I went out fishing on Mr Thomas's boat, one of the typical local boats with a big wheelhouse astern and a small cabin, warm and stuffy, below deck. It was a calm night and it was pleasant drifting off Chapel Point. But when the nets were pulled in it was a poor catch. In the fifties fishing was already in decline but even so Mevagissey still had a sizeable fleet. Now, in summer at least, the fishing is more of a token – a saleable element in another industry altogether, tourism.

Carrick Roads and King Harry Ferry

The elegant, richly carved and clover-leaf-shaped castle at St Mawes is one of a pair guarding the entrance to Carrick Roads. These waters are exceptionally beautiful and peaceful. At high tide the herons flap away, the dark rocks at the water's edge disappear and the dense foliage of the woodland seems to brush the water. These inlets are deep and sheltered and have provided a safe long-term anchorage for big ships; they were used during the war by the invasion fleet preparing for the Normandy landings. But when I saw them they were filled with unwanted drilling-rigs, old Channel ferries, Falklands troopships and curiously-named oil tankers. Just upstream from King Harry Ferry there is a pretty thatched pub with a figurehead at the water's edge and a perfect view of this oddly assorted and thought-provoking fleet. Nearby was another vessel with a message for this country's industry: a monster bulk carrier used to bring Japanese cars here from half-way round the world: an invasion that all the cannon of St Mawes Castle are powerless to check.

St Mawes Castle

Carrick Roads from Messack

The Fal near King Harry Ferry

Charlestown

Bayard's Cove, Dartmouth

Charlestown, Plymouth, Dartmouth and Torquay

Charlestown near St Austell is an instance of imaginative preservation: a narrow dock with lock-gates and a seawall, backed by a row of modest cottages and still in use as a china-clay port. Although it is not big, the handsome quayside is complicated in structure and was built by Smeaton, who also built the stone pier at St Ives and the old Eddystone lighthouse which now stands on Plymouth Hoe. Another historically and architecturally interesting remnant at Plymouth is the quayside of the old Barbican. Its handsome and substantial warehouses, while adapting to the times – Sally's Crêperie, wine bar, electrostatics firm, tavern and restaurant – have avoided wholesale gentrification. Outside the working fish market Cap'n Jasper's does 10p mugs of tea and baked potatoes. None of this would do at all on the nicely cobbled and historic quayside of Bayard's Cove at Dartmouth, an old and fastidiously maintained cul-de-sac. It is an extension of the busy main Dartmouth waterfront, itself laden with discreet but substantial Victorian and Edwardian splendour.

But even sedate Dartmouth is under pressure, with the prospect of a large deep-water port in the Dart. The Brixham waterfront is lively and unashamedly commercial. Its fishing tackle and gift shops, pubs, shell shop, crab shop and restaurants form a backdrop for an enticing and breathless row of ticket booths offering day trips: 'Come wreck-fishing on *Sea Spray*, free bait tea coffee.' At one end of the quayside, cranes and excavators are at work on an enormous new jetty; at the other end lies a small half-submerged fishing boat next to a black replica of the *Golden Hind*. This replica itself sank at sea when under tow recently.

Torquay is something else again: a handsome Victorian and Edwardian centre, like Dartmouth, but sinking architecturally under the weight of the ever-more-conspicuous late-twentieth-century additions. It is also a rather touching place early in the season, with lines of mainly retired people sitting close-packed, shoulder to shoulder, enjoying the fitful spring sun on the benches under the dusty palms.

The Barbican, Plymouth

Brixham

Torquay

Mill Bay, Salcombe

The Dart at Dartmouth

Sandstone cliffs at Dawlish

Dawlish

South Devon and Lyme Regis

Brunel's Great Western Railway was a mixed blessing to South
Devon, opening it up and making it prosperous, but at a certain
price. The nearest the Great Western ever got to Salcombe was
Kingsbridge, six miles away. Teignmouth and Dawlish, though,
are on the main line. At Dawlish this is luckier for the passengers
than for anyone else; they can enjoy the magnificent shore scenery
and the fun of hurtling through tunnels in the red sandstone cliffs
only a few hours out of Paddington, whereas Dawlish's beach
could well do without the railway altogether.

My first childhood visit to Lyme Regis was also made by train.
A delightfully picturesque and big-domed steam engine, an
antique even then, with plenty of shining brass, pulled a short
train up and down the pretty but long-vanished line from
Axminster Junction. It was wartime; Lyme had by then grown
shabby and unpainted and run-down; it was Easter and the sea
was still cold. There was nothing to do in the town. But there was
the Cobb (the sinuous breakwater and harbour wall) to wander
on and to draw, stretches of beach and undercliff to explore, and
walks along sandy cliff paths between thickets of gorse where one
might see basking adders flicker out of the sunlight into the dark
brambles. Looking back on them, those weeks seem as perfect as
a holiday could be. The town is brightened up a lot now but the
Cobb seems little different.

Teignmouth

Lyme Regis: The Cobb   Below: Lyme Regis

Durdle Door

Durdle Door is, like Bedruthan Steps, the remarkable result of erosion of soft rocks leaving behind a harder structure, in this instance an archway of Portland stone. The rock strata, instead of lying in flat layers, are up-ended and curved as if they were layers of pastry instead of hard stone. The approach to Durdle Door is memorable: through a caravan site set in a grove of Scotch pines and across a steep downland slope which is itself crested by a line of caravans, like the foam of a breaking wave. If you look straight ahead, Durdle Door is an undisputed beauty spot. If you take in the scene as a whole it is a good example of the inevitable and increasing tensions between protecting the coastline and giving market forces free rein.

West Bay

West Bay and Portland Bill

There are two especially noticeable kinds of stone to be seen on the Dorset coast. Its golden sandstone appears most conspicuously at the top of Golden Cap, but most spectacularly in the line of cliffs that stretches east from West Bay near Bridport, worn away and battered into strange shapes by the same waves that make fleeting patterns of foam on the shingle.

Beyond lies Chesil Beach, and at its far end rises the Isle of Portland: a desolate place with a naval barracks and an equally dismal Borstal, ending in Portland Bill and the jetties from which Portland stone is shipped. The quarries are worth looking at; the stone evidently gets better as it gets deeper. I did this drawing fairly early on in the course of preparing this book, and now regret not having made more of the wooden huts and cafés behind the jetties: not in order to make a critical point, but because if you resolutely cast off your customary blinkers such details are what makes such a seaside scene not simply real but fascinating.

Stone jetties, Portland Bill

159

Studland, Poole and Bournemouth

The best-looking chalk rock stacks I have seen are the Old Harry Rocks at the easternmost point of the Isle of Purbeck. They stand tall and sheer at the end of untouched and pleasant Studland Bay as if to mark the end of the wilder stretches of the south-western coast. Just over the Sandbanks Ferry is the big urban mass of Bournemouth and Poole. The waterfront at Poole is its most interesting section, its quayside still very active, though here as elsewhere the tall warehouses have had to find themselves new jobs. The best-looking Customs House in the country, in Georgian red brick with a circular staircase in front, stands over the road from the quay next to a good maritime museum.

Although some of its pine-shaded suburbs are pretty, it is hard to warm to Bournemouth. The asphalt paths of its wooded chines seem as excessively ordered and metropolitan as the rest of the town, which offers the drawbacks of suburban London without the compensations. White blocks of flats constitute its skyline and every square yard of open space is car park. But on the esplanade at the end of Alum Chine was a surprising vision: an extremely formal stone arcade of shelters supporting a row of very ordinary and un-grand wooden huts, just like Landseer's painting *Dignity and Impudence*. Bournemouth has enough of the one but not of the other.

Bournemouth

Harry Rocks and a Poole warehouse

161

The Isle of Wight: Osborne and Alum Bay

Queen Victoria's bathing machine in the grounds of Osborne House is only a grand version of an object which, invented in Margate in 1753, became a familiar feature of nineteenth-century resorts. The bather undressed in it as it was pulled down the beach into the waves, which could then be entered in privacy. An incidental advantage was that you thus reached deep water instantly, with no chilly wading first. This bathing machine has been moved up from the Solent to retirement amid the flowerbeds and privets, the pines and cedars of the Osborne gardens.

The Isle of Wight's seaside towns have individuality and vitality and have put themselves out for visitors with inventiveness and in some style. In the course of this, much of the natural coastline has either vanished or been turned to account as raw material, its fissured cliffs turned into regulated chines and fantasy theme parks, its marshes into nature reserves. Though there is still an emptier stretch of left-over coastline on the south-west flank, the landscapes I like best on the island are at its western tip: overlooking the Needles and nearby at Alum Bay. Alum (potassium aluminium sulphate was once mined here, as at Hummersea Scar. The cliffs are formed of differently coloured sands, whose contrasting tints are often used to make stripey lighthouses and similar souvenirs. The splendid downland walk from the Alum Bay cliffs round to the Needles Battery has fine views across towards Southampton and the New Forest, with the blue Solent in between.

Queen Victoria's bathing machine, Osborne

cliffs at Alum

The solent

The South Coast

As landscape the south coast has pretty well had it. Above high-tide mark, apart from a few notable stretches of grass, shingle, mud and chalk, suburbia dominates from Bournemouth to Margate. For most of the way you can see the shore from the car. Looking to landward from the beach, the typical view is of a busy road backed by Victorian and Edwardian terraces or by thirties villas and semis, with high-rise flats as a backdrop. As townscape and beach scenery, however, it is varied and extremely interesting, since the whole history of the seaside – from its virginal beginnings through the splendours of its middle years to its present raddled decadence – is here spread out.

The south coast, more than any of the others, is an expression of, or monument to, everybody's simple wish to get near the sea. As the stretch of shore nearest to London it attracted first the Prince Regent, then the middle-class holidaymakers, and now the commuters, becoming by degrees the most commercial and most developed coastline of them all. A bus ride along it is on the landward side at least a completely urban or suburban experience, though often relieved by the openness on the other side. The older towns are no longer isolated units but simply the focal points, the bits with the nice terraces and the bus stations and the multi-storey this-and-thats. Their outskirts thinning out first into classy green-tiled thirties villas and then into unambitious semis, are drearily repetitive because everyone needed the same thing; even in the thirties, before anyone had heard of 'productivity', variety was already expensive.

The notable, spectacular surprises of this coast are the big power-stations (Portslade, near Hove; Dungeness), and in eastern Kent the vast parking areas for newly shipped-in cars. Architecturally its most rewarding aspects, after the famous sea-front splendours of Brighton and Hove, can be found in the indestructible character and individuality of the various towns (the Brighton Lanes, Deal, Margate) if you explore behind their esplanade façades.

The south coast is the one nearest to France and to foreigners and is therefore heavily sprinkled with defences of various sorts; some, like the military canal and the Martello towers, now looking pathetically ineffectual and a bit panicky; others, at Rye, Deal, Camber, Portsmouth, efficiently meeting clear if improbable threats. Portsmouth and Chatham are fascinating for their odd mixtures of the historic, the picturesque, the elegant and the deadly. But, Southampton apart, the mercantile quaysides do not seem particularly historic – being so busy, they are rebuilt continually. And not much provision was ever made for the smaller working boats along this coast: they were simply hauled up the shingle, as they are still at Bognor and Worthing, Hastings and Hythe. The visible signs of the old fishing industries of Hastings and Rye are not quaysides but tarred net- and sail-sheds.

The most interesting historical remains along this southern shore are not military or industrial but commercial, relating to the archaeology of the seaside as an English institution. Its monuments are the fine terraces, esplanades and piers, the beach tramways and cliff railways, the amusement halls and the gin palaces. Its awful warnings are seen in the greedy and uncontrolled sprawl of the middle decades of this century, abated now that there is nowhere left to build, and in the inadequacy of the planners. Recent additions do not inspire hope. There are raw gaps along the seafront filled by car parks, fun-lands and conference centres; hotels, once-elegant, have vulgarized their façades by turning them into strident self-promotional hoardings. And even where a terrace keeps itself meticulously orderly, it cannot control its surroundings. The terraces of Brighton and Hove have the same grandeur as Bath's when seen in close-up, but looking back at them from the pier they are now insignificant, swamped by the high-rise blocks behind. Other sea-fronts – Bognor, Deal – have no high-rises and have kept their identity intact.

There are splendid walks along the south coast: up and down the slopes of the Seven Sisters or along the shore at their feet, up on top of the same grey chalk at Beachy Head or over the South Foreland at Dover; plodding laboriously along through the Dungeness shingle among the strange cabbagy clumps of greenery, enjoying the irrepressible sparkiness of the tacky bungalows plonked down in front of the nuclear power-stations. The oddest place along this entire coast is the half-natural, half-man-made shore at Dymchurch Steps. The straight and endless sloping concrete of the seawall, and the regularity of the groynes in the sand evenly diminishing to their vanishing point, make the whole scene look like an art student's perspective exercise. Paul Nash painted it memorably, making the browny-grey waves as solid and heavy as the concrete shore itself. In winter it is eerily deserted and lonely, like Dungeness. But in summer the south-coast beaches fill up with fishermen and lobster-coloured sunbathers, bright nylon windshields and Punch and Judies, and you can see the English coastline looking as resilient as ever – dirty, crowded, vulgar, lively and fun.

Southampton, Buckler's Hard, Beaulieu and Bosham

At Southampton you no longer board an Atlantic greyhound for Cherbourg and New York: only the ferry for Cowes. This gives the long quay an undeniably nostalgic and pointless feel, as if at a deserted airport. Its grander remnants, like this tall warehouse and the proudly domed pierhead building beyond, now look increasingly isolated as the quays around them become car parks prior to being cleared for office building.

At Buckler's Hard, the woodland shipbuilding village on the Beaulieu River, the emphasis is not on nostalgia but on a sense of history. A good maritime museum and imaginative reconstructions in some of the eighteenth-century cottages offer at least an impression of the shipbuilding industry that once gave this place its being. The waterfront has two aspects, one a prosperous-looking boatyard, the other an evocative relic of the past with weathered wooden piling and an old steam launch. From here

Southampton

Bucklers Hard

Beaulieu

Bosham

there is a boat trip down through the moored yachts and the still
pleasantly wooded landscape to where the Beaulieu River
broadens into the Solent, or a walk upstream by the narrowing
river to the village of Beaulieu, where the riverside trees and the
wet mud are beautiful in the autumnal quiet.

Bosham is more active. Even in late October when the Channel
is emptying of boats, the car park behind its tranquil waterfront
still suggests a village almost entirely dedicated to sailing. It is a
pretty place; its colours, like Buckler's Hard's, are those of brick
and tile and white paint. But, apart from their similar colours and
similar situations on secluded waters, they are very different: the
one vigorously conserved as a splendid museum piece, the other a
beauty spot which is nevertheless also a going concern.

Bosham Creek

Portsmouth

Two different navies are on display at Portsmouth: the picturesque and historic navy, its charms enhanced and its brutal disciplines made more tolerable by the passage of time; and the grey and businesslike navy of today. This last is the one you see during the harbour boat trip, its ships bristling with incomprehensible weaponry but the metal skins stretched over their skeleton structure looking thin and vulnerable none the less. The guides who show you round Nelson's *Victory* are proper sailors who speak of the harshness of the bad old days with a certain grisly relish; the heavy timbers, the lack of headroom, the guns and the gloom make it all too comprehensible. The elegance or even prettiness of Nelson's and Hardy's quarters above all this make a curious contrast, all the more striking for their close proximity to the lower decks.

It is odd and rather moving to see many of the wooden structural details of the *Victory* clearly foreshadowed in the doomed Mary Rose of two centuries earlier.

Portsmouth dockyard is full of fascinating relics, structural, architectural and decorative. The old town nearby has some fine eighteenth-century houses and also the solid Tudor Round Tower built for Henry V. The harbour trip is interesting both for the various ships you pass and for the chance to see the Portsmouth and Gosport waterfronts from a distance, looking like thin strips of painted scenery.

Bognor Regis

Despite its funny name Bognor is rather nice. I took the train there quite early one spring Saturday with my seven-year-old son, who went off by himself for trips on the esplanade tramway and on various similar harmless excursions while I drew. Now and then he drew too, looking carefully at the shapes of boats and huts and bandstand. We had sandwiches from a sandwich bar for elevenses on the beach, lunch at the pierhead fish-and-chips bar, tea at an open-verandahed café on the front, and supper at a Wimpy. In between we talked to a friendly off-duty fortune-teller who was enjoying the spring sun with her friends, had a mid-afternoon rest on the shingle, and walked along the shore to Aldwick, where the sand suddenly seems to become merely an extension of the back gardens of the close-packed houses which overlook it – there is no beach road. The beach huts we passed on the way were good specimens: old, solid, weathered, soft-coloured and sun-bleached, and backed by a sandy footpath shaded by tamarisks. All the seafront buildings were quite low, which gave the town a strangely old-fashioned appearance. There was a pleasant spindly iron bandstand and plenty of wooden groynes curving up with the shape of the beach; in the evening someone was sitting on one of them and fishing. We both got red from the sun and the wind and caught the train back to London worn out after a good day.

Bognor from the pier

GET YOUR DECK CHAIR HERE

The front at Bognor

Worthing

Worthing, Hove and Brighton

Worthing's Marine Parade terraces are medium-sized; elegant but domestic. In parts they have kept the original unity of their façades. They overlook a pleasant pebble-and-seaweed beach, only held in place by the heavy wooden groynes. You can sense the immense pull of the beach tides from the way the stones are piled high on the west side of each and scooped out deeply on the east. The 'New Amusements' hall on the pier is in full-blooded thirties idiom, all the corners rounded off but the clock-faces perversely squared. Until 1798 Worthing was merely a simple row of fishing cottages. On the beach to the east of the town, surrounded by the timber-built boats and the long rows of boarded huts, you can still almost imagine it as it then was.

The bus journey from here to Brighton takes you along Worthing's extensive lines of semi-detached villas from the

Worthing

HOVE

1900s and the 1930s and past the biggest landmark on the Sussex coast, the power-station at Portslade, before coming eventually to the spectacular Brunswick Terrace at Hove. This was built in the 1820s on the same scale as Nash's Cumberland Terrace in Regent's Park. Buildings as big as this need an open space like a park or a seashore in front of them to be properly seen. By contrast, the pretty and uproariously decorative wooden arcade

at the far end of the Palace Pier at Brighton is best seen from very close up. Like the Brunswick Terrace façade it too is a production-line job, but the units are individually intriguing in their blend of fretwork, boxed-in carpentry and exuberant pseudo-Islamic inventiveness. This is a structure which carries to its extreme the delightful wood-and-white-paint vernacular found all along the south coast.

Palace Pier

Brighton: Palace Pier and West Pier

Brighton has two piers. One, the Palace Pier, is currently a going concern, crude but vital. The other, the West Pier, is a pale ghost, less inventive but more careful and scrupulous about its borrowings. The Palace Pier of 1899 is the showman's equivalent of the Royal Pavilion, the decorative inspiration for its arches and domes coming from Indian motifs but transformed by enthusiasm and the need to get things built in a solid way without fussing.

Seen from the shore (which is as near as you can now get)

the West Pier's far pavilions look more architectural and more painstakingly detailed. There are pretty echoes of Udaipur and the Raj and of the curved roof of the Paris Grand Palais. This devastated and embattled pier was once used to make the film of *Oh, What A Lovely War!*, and there is still a great deal of inpenetrable barbed wire about in order to deter patrols. It is sadly run down and defeat is looming: it would surely be worth one final Big Push to save it.

West Pier

On the whole, the grandest Brighton terraces are straight,
though not level, but Hove's Adelaide Crescent (*over the page*)
bends sinuously and elegantly back and forth as it approaches
the seafront. Here, as in Belgravia, the white and shining façades
sometimes remind me of chalk cliffs – particularly those
of the Seven Sisters, fifteen miles to the east.

Adelaide Crescent, Hove

Cuckmere Haven

Bexhill, The De La Warr Pavilion

The seafront, Bexhill

Hastings

Bexhill and Hastings

Bexhill is renowed, architecturally at least, for the De La Warr
Pavilion, designed by Erich Mendelsohn and built in 1935, an
important precursor in this country of the modern movement.
Its fifty-odd years hardly show. It looks intelligent, elegant, well
maintained and well used. What I had not expected was its
odd situation, above and behind a loyal and celebratory esplanade
shelter. As a telegraphese inscription explains, this was ERECTED
MCMXI KING GEORGE V CORONATION YEAR, and its white
colonnade looks like a funny old bit of wedding cake turned inside
out. It's unusual to see the native and stuffy aspects of Britain so
vividly juxtaposed with the forward-looking European tradition
of only a couple of decades later.

Hastings occupies an unusual seaside situation not at the top
but at the bottom of some cliffs: these provide an individual
backdrop for its most familiar views. The town has its grand

aspects; in particular, Pelham Crescent, a fine curving terrace with
two tiers of bow windows and a handsome central portico, the
whole thing set back majestically above a down-to-earth street-
level row comprising Humbug and Gift shop, fast-food takeaway,
Hastings Rock Shop and the like. I prefer the old town with the
wet fish shops, net-drying huts and the beach and cliff railways:
this last especially should not be missed. As the carriage rises up
the cliff-face, the net-sheds and indeed the whole waterside below
sink and shrink to model scale and take on a rather down-at-heel
appearance. But back at ground level I forgot all this as I noticed
the many beach activities – boats, winches, the burning of tarry
rubbish – and the oddity of the tall clustered net-sheds. No one
looking at Hastings today would think it had ever been one of the
fierce Cinque Ports appointed by the medieval kings to ward off
attacks from France.

181

Dungeness

Dungeness is at the point of a big flat triangle of land poking south into the Channel. Its beach is of shingle which makes walking rather a slog. It is dominated by the big concrete blocks of Dungeness A and B which, as architecture, look to be in a state of Topsy-like growth. The smaller details of the beach are more interesting to look at: the fishing boats and their gear, and the trolleys for their gas cylinders which trundle on track discarded by the miniature railway; and the old tins, cars, anchors, bits of net, railway vans, tarpaulin, winches, driftwood, corrugated-iron huts and greenery which are strewn haphazardly around or just grow up through the pebbles. There are also two lighthouses: one of the old (1904) brick ones, painted black, and an elegant black-and-white concrete one with a spiral base, of 1961. I particularly like the line of bungalows along the road, several hundred yards back from the beach. They are lightly, even tackily, built but durable and cheered up by bits of bright paintwork and home-made signs offering bait, fishing tackle, drinks, crisps, etc., with arrows carefully added to point you towards the right shack.

The beach at Dungeness

Martello Towers at Hythe

New Romney, Hythe, Sandwich and Deal

New Romney, Hythe, Sandwich and Dover (pp. 186–7) are, with Hastings, the ancient Cinque Ports. Romney lies between Dungeness and Romney Marsh; I remember the name of the Romney, Hythe and Dymchurch Railway from early childhood, and took a first ride on it not long ago. The beautiful replica steam engines run from Hythe as far as Romney; from there on to Dungeness, humbler and more utilitarian diesels take over. Hythe stands at the end of a long curving stretch of beach thick with military associations: Martello towers from Napoleonic times, firing ranges still in use. The fishing boats drawn up on its beach have the distinctive overhanging stern typical of this stretch of the south coast. Sandwich, like Romney and the old town centre of Hythe, now stands well inland from the proper sea, on the River Stour, still navigable though partially silted up. On the town side of the river is the sixteenth-century Barbican Gate; through its arch can be seen the old houses which still make up much of the town's centre.

The most interesting surviving seafront in Kent is at Deal. The skyline seen from the end of the pier is low and regular, unbroken by any tall buildings. Fortunately for artists the beach is of shingle, without any sand. This fact has preserved intact the town's largely eighteenth-century waterfront, which would certainly have been swept away by Victorian developers if there had been a sandy beach of the kind families with children need. As it is, Deal's waterfront reminds me of the low flat seaside towns to be seen across the Channel. Deal Castle is a geometrical structure, surprisingly complicated for 1540, surrounded by a dry moat, and bristling, originally at any rate, with 145 cannon. Once you've noticed its anguished face, however, it is hard to imagine the castle being taken seriously. Deal and Walmer melt into one another: Walmer's beach has a lifeboat and plenty more of the white-painted clinker-built fishing boats and the oil-blackened winch engines that give English shingle beaches their unmistakably practical flavour.

Deal from the pier

Deal Castle

The Barbican Gate, Sandwich

The Romney, Hythe and Dymchurch

185

Dover · The South Foreland

188

Broadstairs and Ramsgate

There is a beautiful painting of Pegwell Bay at Ramsgate by the pre-Raphaelite artist William Dyce. Three voluminously clad women and a child with a spade are standing at low-tide among chalky rock-pools; beyond them are some other smaller figures and three donkeys at the foot of a line of low cliffs. Eight years earlier, Dickens – who liked Pegwell Bay – had written *David Copperfield* in nearby Broadstairs, in a castellated house overlooking Viking Bay. If Dickens could see the Broadstairs beach today he might be momentarily surprised by all the bodies

but he would have no difficulty in recognizing the faces.

No bodies, only bodywork, can be seen on the new Sally Viking beach between Ramsgate Harbour and Pegwell Bay's abandoned Hoverport. This used to be a pleasant beach to walk along, with its rock-pools and lumps of chalk, fossils and bits of sand. Now the only sand is dumped in small heaps beside the concrete mixers. There are no sounds of children and no seagulls, only the farting of exhaust pipes and the smell of oil and tar. Britain's long coastline could do without any more beaches like this.

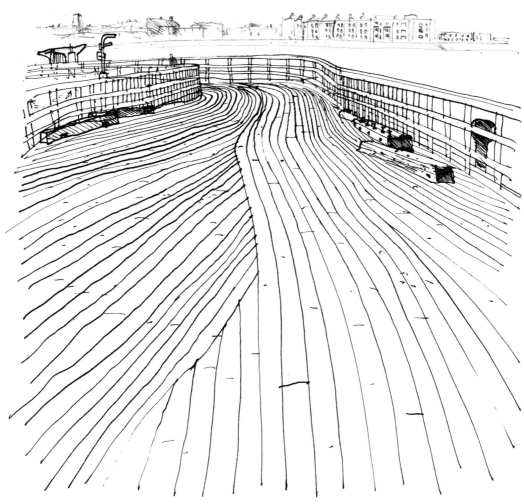

Walton-on-the-Naze

Index